6

CONTEMPORARY LATIN AMERICAN CLASSICS

J. Cary Davis, *General Editor*

MEN *and*
ANGELS

Three South American Comedies

TRANSLATED AND WITH AN INTRODUCTION BY
Willis Knapp Jones

FOREWORD BY *J. Cary Davis*

SOUTHERN ILLINOIS UNIVERSITY PRESS
Carbondale and Edwardsville
FEFFER & SIMONS, INC.
London and Amsterdam

For Polly

ITS FIRST READER WHO
SHARES WITH ME
ENJOYMENT OF A GOOD PLAY

CONTENTS

WILLIS KNAPP JONES received his A.B. degree from Hamilton College in 1917, the A.M. from Penn State in 1922, the Ph.D. (in Romance Languages) from the University of Chicago (1927). He also studied at the University of Chile (1918, 1942) and at the Centro de Estudios Históricos, Madrid (1922).

His scholarly teaching career includes the Instituto Inglés (Santiago, Chile, 1917–19), North American Academy (Montevideo, 1919–20), Penn State (1920–22), and Miami University, Oxford, Ohio, from 1922 until retirement in 1962. During some of this period he was on leave to teach abroad at the U. S. Army College in Shrivenham, England (1947), and at the University of Guayaquil, Ecuador (1948). In addition, he has taught summer courses in the Universities of Wyoming, New Mexico, and Houston. He has twice been Visiting Professor in Spanish at Southern Illinois University (1968, 1969).

Professor Jones was president of the American Association of Teachers of Spanish and Portuguese in 1941; his doctoral thesis on the Spanish Picaresque novel won the La Prensa (N. Y.) prize in 1927. He is a member of the Casa de Cultura Ecuatoriana, and has the Eloy Alfaro medal awarded by the Republic of Panama.

His translations of full-length plays by René Marqués, Armando Moock, Isidora Aguirre, José María Rivarola

Matto, Salvador Novo, and others, have appeared in *Poet Lore*. Among his outstanding contributions in this line, in book form, are *Short Plays of the Southern Americas* (Stanford University, 1944), *Representative Plays of Florencio Sánchez* (Pan American Union, 1961), *One Act Plays from Spain* (Texas, 1936), and the two volume *Spanish American Literature in Translation* (Ungar, 1963–66).

Among his many textbooks, perhaps the most important is a history of the Latin American Theater, titled *Behind Spanish American Footlights* (University of Texas Press, 1966). One of the most recent works, and best, is *Manuela*, the English translation of Demetrio Aguilera Malta's absorbing historical novel, *La caballeresa del sol* (Southern Illinois University Press, 1967).

The trio of plays in the present volume marks the 100th of Professor Jones' copyrighted publications, not including the numerous articles in books and magazines. The list includes textbooks, translations of novels, poems, short stories, plays (from many languages), pamphlets, paper backs, and even songs. Of the last mentioned, his *Five South American Nocturnes* (set to music by Joseph W. Closkey, with Spanish words provided by the Cuban poetess Amparo Rodríguez Vidal, and published by C. C. Birchard) sold more than 30,800 copies in the last twenty years. Another song, *A Bird Flew*, sold 146,744 copies in thirty years.

Jones' acquaintance with the South American Theater is not a bookish one: he has met and corresponded with many of the writers and actors in all these countries. In 1958, he made a trip around South America, visiting the various capitals, seeing plays, talking to actors and playwrights, and giving talks on the North American Theater—none of this sponsored by the U. S. Government. He has known personally the writers represented in this volume, as well as members of their families. In answer to a query about "cold maté," Rivarola Matto mailed him a maté gourd, *bombilla,* and maté powder with directions for mixing it. They had met and

talked in Asunción about plays and ambitions. His correspondence with the team of Darthés and Damel began
twenty years ago. The two have sent him many plays and
clippings, and wanted him to select a "more serious" drama
than *La hermana Josefina* for this volume. Professor Jones
treasures a copy of one of Samuel Eichelbaum's "lost" plays,
typed and sent to him by the playwright's daughter.

In this collection of plays, we have a representative selection from the modern theater in three South American countries: Chile, Argentina, and Paraguay. These plays are not
heavy reading, yet each presents an interesting picture of
contemporary society in each region. They do not necessarily
"have a message"—they are strictly meant to be entertaining,
and it is hoped that the reader finds them so.

Professor Jones' "Introduction" provides a brief but
comprehensive summary of the Spanish American Theater to
date. The reader who is interested in further study should
find the Checklist of Translations useful.

J. Cary Davis

Southern Illinois University
January 1970

INTRODUCTION

UNLIKE DRAMA in Spain, which for a long time dealt only with religious themes, the early theater of Spanish America included both religious and popular material. Of course theatrical performances began four hundred years after Spain's twelfth century *Auto de los reyes magos* (Play of the Magis), and by then nonreligious elements had long been part of the peninsular theater. But the earliest performances in the New World, *The Shepherd Play,* performed under the direction of priests in Cortés's expedition for the religious instruction of the Indians, included one shepherd bringing a butter tub in which to bathe the Baby Jesus, another who had eaten the tamales he was bringing as a present and could offer the Christ Child nothing but a song, and a local hermit with a rosary of spools. And as they left, they called back: "Goodbye, Aunt Mary; So long, Uncle Joe!" This same mixture of the sacred and profane continued in later New World plays.

The first Spanish conquerors had found no tradition of dramatic exhibitions among the Indian inhabitants in any way resembling European performances. True, Cortés in Mexico, Pedro de Acosta in Peru, and other explorers elsewhere described stages erected in the plazas of Indian villages, but they served only as platforms for dances to pray for good crops, and for pantomimes reenacting events in the history of the inhabitants. Though practically all the elements of drama were to be found in one part or another of the hemisphere, scholars assert that nowhere were they put together to resemble European plays.

Thus America's first dramatic performances were based on scripts brought from Spain or written by priests following Spanish models. Practically all of the earlier ones used bible stories; the remainder were based on European themes or Indian events. The earliest mention of one, though without giving its title, occurs in the records of the Mexican cabildo, or council, under date of January 9, 1526. The minutes of the meeting speak of payment for a production of what was probably an Epiphany play, three days earlier. Other performances in Mexico quickly followed. The titles—*Representation of the End of the World, The Fall of Our First Parents,* and one performed in the Nahuatl language in 1536, *The Last Judgment*—testify to their biblical character.

In another part of the hemisphere, and as early as January 6, 1544, Padre Lezcano took the first steps in Paraguay's theatrical history with what must have been a shepherd play performed in front of the Asunción Cathedral. It will be discussed in the special section on Paraguay. Comedies directly imported from Spain were performed in Ecuador in 1550 and 1568, while in 1580 for the entertainment of visiting bishops in Bogotá, Colombia, Archbishop Zapata staged *Los Alarcos,* a tragic story frequently used by later dramatists. It tells of a Spanish princess who ordered Count Alarcos to kill his wife so that he could be free to marry the princess.

The next step was the abandonment of European material in favor of New World plots. Investigators not long ago came upon a short play by Cristóbal de Llerena, performed in Santo Domingo, June 3, 1588. It contained so violent a denunciation of church and government officials that its author was pulled out of bed and shipped into exile as soon as orders could be prepared.

With the passing of time, plays based on American legends and history became rather common. In 1693, Chileans welcomed their new governor and his Peruvian bride with a performance in Concepción of *The Chilean Hercules* which, in its dramatization of the colonists' struggles against the Araucanian Indians, warned him of what awaited him. War also motivated the first known play in Uruguay, a boastful account of victory. It was titled *Purest Loyalty and Buenos Aires Avenged*, and came from the pen of Juan Francisco Martínez, chaplain of the troops from Montevideo. Mars, representative of the Argentine army, is congratulated by Argentine and Uruguayan women for his defeat of the British Neptune. Originally the idea was to clothe the chorus of women in army uniforms, but the idea of women in men's clothes on the stage was so shocking to the censor that he ordered them to appear in the more revealing but less censorable costumes of nymphs.

In general, however, between the discovery of America and the struggle of the Spanish colonists for their independence, not many local dramatists were given a hearing. What few plays were presented in Latin America's centers of culture, though performed by local amateurs, were imported from Spain.

The occasions for dramatic performances were largely celebrations of important events in Spain, like royal birthdays or weddings, and ceremonies during which men were required to swear loyalty and allegiance to a new sovereign. Also, of more immediate concern, the colonists seized upon the arrival of a new governor or some high church official to mount a welcoming ceremony, complete with a review of troops and a play. Again, the play was likely to be a stage hit from Madrid, brought by galleon, and four or five months en route. Occasionally a local drama enthusiast was allowed to write the introductory *loa* or greeting and praise, and sometimes a brief skit to be played between the acts.

Rarely were Latin Americans lucky enough to welcome a traveling company of actors from the Peninsula. But they did come occasionally. The first troupe with its repertory of early Golden Age *comedias* took to the road when in May,

1598 the pious Philip issued an edict closing "those immoral theatres of Spain." Francisco Pérez de Robles, his wife, and a half dozen other barnstormers dared to cross the ocean and turned up in Lima, Peru, in 1599 to introduce to America the plays of Spain's Lope de Vega.

Mexico as a center of culture was at first the scene of the greatest theatrical activity in the New World. So it deserves some discussion, even if no plays from that country are included in this book. Then Lima assumed importance. After the independence of Spanish America, Argentina and Chile played an increasing role, but nowhere, till recently, were the plays very numerous or of very high dramatic quality.

Mexico

WHEN DISCUSSING early Mexican stage history, historians usually drop the name of Juan Ruiz de Alarcón (1581–1639), a great early Mexican dramatist, since he was born in Mexico. But he lived largely in Spain and there is no proof that he ever wrote plays in his homeland. The "Mexican element," which some critics claim to find in his two dozen plays known to have been written in Spain, is most nebulous. Therefore he seems to belong more fittingly among the three other great names of Spain's Golden Age of drama, Lope de Vega, Tirso de Molina, and Calderón.

Historians of Mexico's theater can with more justice claim the drama of Sor Juana de la Cruz (1648–95), the most intellectual woman of the early New World. However, the few dramatic productions of this learned nun are largely imitations of Lope's cape-and-sword romances or Spanish religious plays, with only two or three original skits embodying Mexican elements inserted between the acts of longer plays.

A still later contributor to Mexico's theatrical movement was the Spain-born Eusebio Vela (1689–1736), from Toledo, who came to Mexico with his brother, under contract to manage a playhouse for the benefit of the Hospitalers. For his actors he wrote a dozen plays, again imitations of Golden Age drama. Their admirers declared them the equal of anything by Lope or Calderón.

In the nineteenth century one figure among Mexican dramatists was Manuel Eduardo de Gorostiza (1789–1851). He could claim to be Mexican only because his mother, wife of the Spanish governor of Vera Cruz, landed in the New World a week before Manuel made his entrance on the scene. And the future playwright left Mexico with his parents before he was six, to write the greater part of his sixty-seven plays, mostly neoclassic, in Spain and England. However, he did come back to Mexico in 1832 where he sold farm machinery, took charge of the national library, managed the Teatro Santa Ana, and died honored as "the restorer of Mexican drama."

Actually it was the Romantic Movement that was responsible for Mexico's first authentic playwright and for injecting new life into the Mexican theater. Ignacio Rodríguez Galván (1816–42), a romanticist in life as well as in writing, went to work in his uncle's book store in Mexico City at a time when the Romantic Movement was thriving in France and Spain. On the shelves he found Romantic French poetry and Romantic Spanish plays to be read in his leisure hours. Inspired by them he wrote two Romantic plays, both based on legend. The first, *Muñoz, visitador de México* (Muñoz, the Royal Inspector) was performed in 1838 and declared "the first Mexican historical drama written by a Mexican." It was set during the conspiracy of 1566, and narrated with considerable poetic license. In it, the Royal Inspector is less interested in the conspirator than in the man's wife. When he accomplishes the death of Sotelo and tells Celestina that she is now free to marry him, she falls dead. Rodríguez Galván's other long tragedy *El privado del rey* (The Royal Favorite,

1842) is a melodrama of violence and devil-possessed characters, based on a story from Juan Manuel of fourteenth-century Spain.

The second important Mexican writer of Romantic plays is Fernando Calderón (1809–45) (not related to the Golden Age dramatist). Because he lived in Zacatecas, he did not make his theatrical debut in the capital quite so early. He started with neoclassic plays which were performed in Zacatecas and Guadalajara. In one of them, *La muerte de Virginia por la libertad de Roma* (The Death of Virginia for the Freedom of Rome, 1832) treating a dramatic happening in Rome of the fifth century B.C., Santa Ana read an attack on his own suppression of civil liberty. Calderón found it expedient to move to Mexico City where, inspired by *Muñoz, visitador de México,* he decided to write some Romantic plays. But he was too much awed by Santa Ana to dramatize local legends, so he began with *El torneo* (The Tourney) set in eleventh-century England. It was first performed in Zacatecas in 1839; then in 1842 it served to dedicate the Teatro Principal in Mexico City. He chose safe protagonists for two other romantic tragedies. Anne Boleyn has always been of considerable interest to those of Spanish blood because they consider her a conniving hussy who broke up the marriage of Spanish Catherine of Aragon to Henry VIII. For that reason, and because it was also an excellent historical drama, Calderón's *Ana Bolena* (1839) became very popular. Its success encouraged him to try again, in a third tragedy, this time turning to twelfth-century Austria. *Hernán o la vuelta del cruzado* (Herman or the Return of the Crusader, 1842) has another complicated plot. Herman leaves his sweetheart and goes off to the Crusades. When he gets back, he finds her married to an older man whose illegitimate son Herman turns out to be. There is nothing for the crusader to do but return to the Holy Land.

Many critics lament the fact that neither Rodríguez Galván nor Calderón, both accomplished dramatists, paid any attention to the Mexican scene. Rodríguez Galván died too early. After an unhappy love experience, he sought to forget it all in a diplomatic post abroad, only to die of yellow fever in Havana at the age of twenty-six. Calderón used Mexico as the setting for one play, revealing his satirical ability and his mastery of dramatic technique and flair for dialogue. But it had nothing to do with Romanticism. In 1831 the Spaniard Bretón de los Herreros had written *Marcela o ¿ a cuál de los tres?* (Marcela or Which of the Three?) pointing out Spanish lack of family discipline and the current aping of the French by an independent Spanish widow who is confronted by three matrimonial opportunities. Calderón replied with the neoclassic *A ninguna de los tres* (None of the Three), contrasting the Mexican Antonio with the Frenchified Carlos, and presenting several very affected girls. But he, too, died before he had time to complete additional plays.

No example of Mexico's rich dramatic productions in recent years is included in this collection, which is confined to South America. For one reason, being nearer to the United States, Mexico's dramatists and their works have a better chance of reaching the reading public of the United States. Indeed a number of recent Mexican plays have already been translated into English.

But no one could leave the subject of the theater in Mexico without mentioning Rodolfo Usigli (1905—). In listing the luminaries of the Spanish American theater, he is always accorded a high place. Usigli was an actor at the age of twelve and a drama critic and book author before he was twenty. However, it took him longer to achieve a reputation as a dramatist and get his plays produced, because he had an uncanny ability to anger people. While the group of drama-lovers operating the Teatro de Orientación were glad to stage Usigli's translations of European works, local impresarios turned down his original manuscripts. One, *El gesticulador* (The Grand Gesture), written in 1937, had to wait ten years for a professional production because of its satire on provincial politics and hypocritical heroism. Yet it was good enough to earn him a drama scholarship at Yale.

Only recently has his ability been realized. Ironically, his first original play, the naturalistic tragedy *Medio tono*, interpreted by the great actress María Teresa Montoya in 1937, was disavowed by its author. He said he was more interested in intimate psychology. The prologues and epilogues which he provides, following the example of his idol, George Bernard Shaw, explain his problems and purposes.

When a drama organization in the United States offered a prize in 1960 for the best Latin American play submitted in translation, Usigli's *Función de despedida* (The Farewell Performance, 1949) about the final appearance of an aging actress and a psychological confrontation between her love and her career, won first prize. But his trilogy of "anti-historical" plays dealing with Mexican history is likely to be his best-remembered endeavor. This trio of tragedies concerns the Aztec Cuauhtémoc, Cortés and Marina, and Maximilian and Carlota. *Corona de sombra* (Crown of Shadows, 1943) was the first of the trilogy to be written, but covers the period nearest our own. The author takes issue with the current concept of historians about the ill-fated Austrian-born emperor, and tries to interpret him and Carlota, rather than repeat what biographers have written about them.

In addition to writing plays and criticizing performances, Usigli sandwiched in with his duties as a Mexican diplomat a career of instructing actors and playwrights, and though many of the leading dramatists of today are products of his classes, Usigli is likely to be remembered longer than most of them.

Specifically, this anthology offers plays from three South American nations, Paraguay, Chile, and Argentina. While one would hardly go looking for playwrights in Paraguay, the other two regions have been centers of drama since the sixteenth century.

Paraguay

PARAGUAY's theatrical history, though extending over a long period, is extremely scanty. As mentioned before, it made an early start when Padre Juan Gabriel Lezcano wrote a Corpus Christi play to be performed on the steps of Asunción's cathedral in 1544. In America's first political uprising, the citizens of Asunción had earlier deposed and jailed the *adelantado* or provincial governor, the much-traveled hiker Cabeza de Vaca. So, while following the formula of Spain's religious plays, the priestly author in his version added individual touches and gave vent to his feelings by calling the ex-governor "a scurvy wolf." Other details and local color were included in this short skit to make it a truly national play, and not merely something brought over from Spain.

Investigators have turned up references to a few other early Paraguayan performances, such as one in 1551 to celebrate the wedding of a local official to the daughter of another. But following that moment of life, drama was moribund for centuries. Occasional plays from Spain, like Calderón's *La vida es sueño* (Life is a Dream), and several by Moreto entertained the few citizens of Asunción between 1767 and 1814. In that year, the first of Paraguay's dictators came to power. Dr. Francia, seeing the covetous eyes of his neighbors upon his territory, practically sealed his frontiers and turned Paraguay into a hermit nation. For him, the theater was unnecessary. He even closed most of the schools, explaining: "As long as Mars is watching, Minerva can sleep." During the twenty-six years of the regime of "El Supremo," researchers have found reference to only one produced play.

Dr. Francia's successor, Carlos Antonio López, had different ideas about Paraguay. He wanted his country to enjoy a cultural awakening. He brought in a railroad and installed a telephone system. Then from Uruguay he summoned an Italian architect to build him a beautiful palace, and the Italian threw in a theater. Thereupon, in 1852, López sent his son to Europe to look for someone who could provide plays and direct their performances.

After finding himself a mistress in Paris, the son came upon a third-rate Spanish dramatist, Ildefonso Antonio Bermejo (1820–92), in exile following the Spanish insurrection of 1846. Bermejo was author of half a dozen plays, including *El poder de un falso amigo* (The Power of a False Friend), written in Paris in 1849. With it and an exaggerated opinion of his own ability, Bermejo arrived in Asunción in 1855, where he first founded a newspaper, then a normal school to provide teachers for the expanding educational system, and finally got around to the theater. He began by directing amateur actors in plays by Ramón de la Cruz and Zorrilla, all the while laboring on what he promised would be "a new and original play."

December 4, 1858 was the gala night of the first performance of *Un paraguayo leal* (A Loyal Paraguayan). With its new names and places, and some local color and phrases in the Guaraní Indian language supplied by a local poet, Bermejo hoped no one would recognize the patched-up version of his *False Friend*. That was Bermejo's only contribution to the Paraguayan theater during his seven years of residence in Asunción. Then he left, angry at the "uncouth Paraguayans." Dictator López, however, remained in power until 1862, with his desire for a thriving Paraguayan theater still unsatisfied.

His son and successor, Francisco Solano López, had little time for theaters except the theater of war. His desire to make use of the magnificent army trained by his father involved him first in the War of the Triple Alliance with Brazil and Uruguay against Argentina. One result was a curious three-act comedy by the American Consul in Asunción, Peter Bliss; he wrote it originally in English, and later saw it per-

formed as *La divertida historia de la triple alianza* (1864).
However, after a single performance, Solano López found
himself fighting for the existence of Paraguay. He himself
faced a Triple Alliance because Brazil and Uruguay had
changed sides and joined Argentina. After that, he had no
time for comedy. His replica of La Scala of Milan that he
had begun to build in order to add culture to Paraguay was
never finished, and there were few productions in the small
theater he had included in the palace built for his mistress,
Madame Lynch. By 1870, Marshal Solano López and 90 per
cent of Paraguay's fighting men were dead.

In the next quarter century, though one or two foreign
companies of actors made their way up the Paraná River
from Buenos Aires, the Paraguayan drama lovers had few
memorable occasions. Most of the population, when it had a
choice, preferred musical plays, in any case. Then in 1906
came the first "Bioscopio lírico," of films with phonograph
accompaniment, and the movies began exerting the same le-
thal effect on legitimate drama here as in other countries.
Still, thorough investigators do find details of a few dramatic
performances. The government sponsored some traveling
troupes from Argentina and Uruguay who attempted, somewhat unsuccessfully, to attract audiences by adding to their
repertory a few local plays by Paraguayan dramatists like
Luis Ruffinelli (1889—), Eusebio Aveiro Lugo (1890—),
Arturo Alsina (1897—) Benigno Villa (1901—) and the
indefatigable Josefina Pla (1907—) and her collaborator
Roque Centurión Miranda (1900–1960).

Another important movement brought productions of
plays in the Guaraní Indian language, spoken by half of Paraguay's inhabitants. The chief exponent, in this only nation
in the world with a truly Indian theater, was Julio Correa
(1890–1953). In five years he and his company performed
eleven of his own plays in Guaraní about the problems of the
lower classes, mainly tragedies, marked by authentic dialog
and a sympathy with his characters. His masterpiece was

Carú-pecá (Undernourished, 1933). Several other dramatists in this bilingual nation, including Mrs. Pla, also contributed plays in Guaraní. Then Correa retired and what Paraguayan critics called "a truly national theater" came to its end. By that time Paraguay was involved in another devastating and impoverishing war.

   With the coming of peace and faltering steps toward economic recovery, other local dramatists began writing, especially the French-trained painter Jaime Bestard (1892–1965) and the politician and newspaper editor Juan Ezequiel González Alsina (1919—). Also, remembering the love of the early Paraguayans for musical plays, several dramatists made attempts to provide a few operettas set in the country. When I was in Asunción, I attended a melodic musical play by Dr. Manuel Frutos Pane, with the Guaraní title *Raida Potí* (The Honorable Country Girl). Its music, based on local themes, was played by an orchestra of three harps and three guitars. Dr. Frutos Pane also wrote a number of serious dramas. Other styles of writing were also being used experimentally. Carlos Colombino (1937—), wrote a surrealist one-act play, *Momentos para los tres* (Moments for Three, 1958). Mario Halley Mora (1928—) wrote, performed, and published his modern miracle play *Un traje para Jesús* (A Garment for Jesus). But the play I enjoyed most was something termed "a modern miracle play," by a lawyer turned playwright, Dr. José María Rivarola Matto, (1917—). It is called *El fin de Chipí González* (The Fate of Chipí González, 1954), and is here translated. It is at the same time a fantasy and a realistic picture of life in a lower-class, rural family. The play has recognizable and universal problems: a football son who lives only for sports; a couple of teen-age girls squabbling over him; a farmer troubled by the prices his crops will bring; and a crooked politician who, once given the opportunity, does unto others as he has been done by. The fact that a good angel and a bad devil are included in the cast does not turn the play into a fairy tale. They only serve as a sort of chorus to provide the initial suspense, the "narrative hook," and the concluding philosophy. Besides its atmosphere, redolent of the soil, and its pessimistic picture of corruption at all levels of Paraguayan national life, the play has its philosophical and optimistic moments that lift it above mere entertainment.

Fantasy and sentiment are still characteristic of many plays from Spanish America. I must admit that it is especially visible in the Argentine play included in the anthology. That, however, was written thirty years ago, much nearer the Victorian Age when heroines fainted and strong men dissolved in tears.

I once asked the director of a civic theater in America why she did not schedule more plays from our Pan-American neighbors. "Because they don't get across to North American audiences," was her explanation. "They're too sentimental."

In vain did I point out examples of both sentiment and fantasy that had been successful on Broadway. James Barrie was popular because of his sentimental vein, and a later Barry —Philip—wrote *You and I.* And there was Jean Webster with *Daddy-Long-Legs.* As for fantasy, what about plays starring a mermaid, death sitting in a tree, or a town coming to life one day in a century? "But those were popular in the twenties and thirties," was her refutation. Then what about O'Neill's *Ah, Wilderness!,* or Van Druten's *I Remember Mama,* or if those are also too far in the past, consider Schmidt and Jones' *The Fantastiks,* both sentimental and fantastic but still being performed by college drama groups and even occasionally on T.V.? However, with all the realism, naturalism, and obscenity on the stage of today, about perverts and written for voyeurs, I could not convince her.

I had one more argument and a different approach. Maybe she could start a new trend. In the French theater of the nineties, full of realism, even sordidness, what play ran counter to everything the Parisians were accustomed to seeing? That most popular and sentimental of all plays, Ros-

tand's *Cyrano de Bergerac* in 1898. But she still did not believe that anything from Latin America could have such an
effect on Broadway audiences.

Chile

BECAUSE of the great power of the church in colonial Chile
and its traditional antagonism toward the theater, early writers for the stage who lived there were given little encourage-
ment. Yet there was no objection when "military men, law-
yers, and notables of the realm" staged a theatrical
performance in Santiago in 1633 to celebrate the return to
health of their governor, Laso de la Vega. And to welcome
their new Captain General, Marín de Poveda and his Peruvian bride in 1693, it was considered proper for the social
lights of Concepción in the south to perform in a dramatization of the career of the Araucanian Indian chief, Caupoli-
cán, in *El Hércules chileno* (The Chilean Hercules). But
when the public began talking about a theater to provide
them with a regular fare of plays, the bishops thundered
against the immorality of the theater and most governors listened to them, though some clergy must have looked away
when women performed in Christmas plays. However, the
stage in Chile had one friend. Its Irish governor, Ambrose
O'Higgins, liked to go to the theater; so in 1789, seizing on
the excuse of the coronation of Charles IV, he arranged for a
program of dramas in Santiago. Being the highest authority,
he was safe from clerical protest. But the truth of the
church's accusations was substantiated four years later when
a socially prominent beauty, Josefa Morales, appeared on the
stage and displayed her ankles! As O'Higgins had moved on
to become Viceroy in Peru, actors faced a losing battle for existence.

With independence won from Spain in 1818, the theater,
under Bernardo O'Higgins, illegitimate son of the old governor, won a new lease on life. Leaders of the new republic de-

clared the stage an educational adjunct of the schools; therefore money was provided for a playhouse in Santiago and actors were assembled for a new season. All but two of the actors were recruited from among the prisoners of war, and some of the patriotic Chilean ladies offered to become the actresses. But it was not so easy to find dramatists. Those who did present scripts were more apt to ape the plays of Spain than to attempt anything original set in the Chile with which they were more familiar. And most of them, in their attempts to be educational, forgot they also had to provide conflict and drama to keep their audiences awake.

What changed this situation was the performance in Copiapó, Chile, in 1857, of a Spanish zarzuela or musical comedy based on a Spanish episode. Back in Spain, dramatists had been experimenting with a new type of play intending to give different regions of the nation some idea of what their more distant countrymen were like. And so plays were written about regional dances or customs, or even legends and episodes typical of a certain section of the nation. Now, following the performance of such a zarzuela in Copiapó, the touring company continued on to the capital. Chilean playwrights realized how well this type of play could be adapted to Chilean life, and gradually some of them tried it and started working on local-color plays.

One of the greatest of Chile's novelists, Alberto Blest Gana (1830–1920), had hinted at such a possibility with a three-act drama, *El jefe de la familia* (The Head of the Family), published serially in a literary magazine in 1858, but never actually performed till Miguel Frank's company staged it in Santiago a century later.

Another Chilean costumbrista, Daniel Barros Grez (1839–1904) established his position as a Chilean Bretón de los Herreros the next year, by a witty and brief *La beata o los dos matrimonios* (The Religious Woman or the Two Married Couples). He was not quite sure what he intended doing in this satire of women who spend their time at church to the detriment of their home duties, so he called it a "drami-tragi-comic story." He tried again in other plays like *Como en Santiago* (As in Santiago, 1874) that enjoyed a brief popularity and were soon forgotten, though the one named was revived by a Santiago experimental theater in 1947. Its enthusiastic acceptance after a lapse of three quarters of a century, proved the timeliness of its story about the upright *huaso* or cowboy Manuel, the henpecked Don Victoriano, and his wife Ruperta who wanted everything done in their small town just as it was done in Santiago.

Then came a quartet of later costumbristas who had a longer period of popularity than Barros Grez. Earliest was Román Vial y Ureta (1833–96) who began writing ten years after Barros Grez. His first attempt, *Una votación popular* (Election Day, 1869) poked fun at voting in Valparaiso, the satirist's home town. His greatest success, *Choche y Bachicha* (George and the Immigrant, 1870) presents the problem of the Italian immigrant Giuseppe, whose mutilation of the Spanish language brings him trouble in an arson investigation. After the Philadelphia World Fair made the telephone well known, Román Vial wrote *Alo, alo o el teléfono* (1892).

Another Chilean writer of local-color plays was Luis Rodríguez Velasco (1838–1919). His criticism of Chilean high society in his *Por amor o por dinero* (For Love or Money, 1869) brought him notoriety after many in the audiences criticized the means by which the hero Lindor won wealthy María.

Juan Rafael Allende (1850–1909) adhered more closely to the formula of the Spanish zarzuela. He replaced the lower-class servants in the Spanish plays by Chilean *rotos* in such comedies as *Moro viejo* (The Old Moor, 1881) with its unforgettable drunk *roto*, and *José Romero alias Peluca*, about another tough lower-class Chilean. During the War of the Pacific, Allende wrote plays to whip up patriotic frenzy against the Peruvians, but his earlier products are superior.

The fourth of the quartet of costumbristas influenced by

the zarzuela was the university-educated Antonio Espiñeira (1855–1907), whose early plays, especially two with Cervantes as a principal character, might have passed as something written by any of the best of Madrid's playwrights. However, his two-act masterpiece with an untranslatable pun for title, *Chincol en Sartén* (1876), is pure Chilean, involving the rural huaso Chincol, owner of the dog Mustafa, a chip-of-the-old-block, and his poetry competition with Sartén, a *roto* from the city. Sartén's self-confidence brings his own defeat. Another drama, *Lo que no tiene sanción* (Unsanctioned) reveals Espiñeira's interest in psychology.

Of all of Chile's playwrights before the contemporary period, three stand out. Germán Luco Cruchaga (1894–1936) gained immortality with one play, *La viuda de Apablaza* (The Widow of Apablaza, 1927). The widow is a tough old character, running a ranch in the territory of the Araucanian Indians and in love with Nico, the natural son of her dead husband. When she realizes that he loves her niece, the sickly schoolteacher Florita, who had come to southern Chile to convalesce, the widow takes herself out of the picture with a shotgun. The author of what has been called one of Chile's three greatest plays decided to attempt a play after witnessing a performance of Florencio Sánchez's *Barranca abajo* (Down the Gully) and to do for Chile what the Uruguayan dramatist had done for the River Plate region. Being a wealthy aristocrat, Luco Cruchaga was under no pressure to continue writing after his one successful experiment.

Second of Chile's dramatists of the period is the self-taught Antonio Acevedo Hernández (1886–1962), born and brought up among the impoverished people of south Chile who figure in most of his writing. Some critics have rated his *Cardo negro* (Black Thistle, 1913) as one of Chile's three greatest plays. They called it the first play to present the Chilean scene realistically without falsification for the sake of either humor or tragedy. Certainly it had a superb beginning, but the second and third acts are weak, and its setting of a provincial town, with village idiot and blind poet, is not typical. It seems crude and bitter, but in most of his fifty plays, Acevedo Hernández showed more force than technique. For his defense of the down-trodden *inquilino* or sharecropper and his attack on other social injustices, he has been labeled leftist, if not Communist. After the first performance of *La canción rota* (The Poor Man's Song, 1921) about the terrible feudal position and eventual revolt of farm hands against a cruel overseer, he was criticized as a nihilist.

In style completely different, Acevedo Hernández wrote amusing skits about the lower-class *rotos* among whom he lived, like *Un 18 típico* (A Typical Independence Day, 1928). As an authority on Chilean folklore, he used some of his material in plays like *Chañarcillo* (1933), full of the legends about a lost mine; in *Joaquín Murieta* (1933), about a Chilean bandit during the California gold rush; and in the sentimental *Arbol viejo* (1934) about a patriarch who sees himself the sturdy oak protecting his family. The dramatist's idyllic *Camino de flores* (Path of Flowers, 1919 and 1929) won the 1934 Santiago Municipal Drama prize during a later revival, and was praised for its spirit reminiscent of Spain's Martínez Sierra. In the last years of his life he wrote little and what he did set down was kept from the public by his protective wife.

If Acevedo Hernández could be likened to Martínez Sierra, Chile's other great dramatist of the period, Armando Moock (1894–1942) wrote with the pen of the Alvarez Quintero brothers. Of the fifty or more plays by him, all but two or three ran for at least one hundred performances. One light skit, *Cuando venga el amor* (When Love Arrives, 1920), caught on in Argentina and enjoyed two thousand performances. Moock went on a barnstorming tour in his *Pueblecito* (The Small Town, 1918); then, snubbed by Chilean critics because he had not come up through journalism like most Chilean dramatists, Moock left his country permanently. First he went to Buenos Aires where in 1921 he had four plays running simultaneously. The delightful *Mocosita* (The Youngster, 1929) though given an Argentine setting, shows by internal evidence that it was conceived in Chile. So it could win a prize in Chile as the best national play of the year and at the same time win honors in Buenos Aires as a typical Argentine comedy.

Moock's amusing *Rigoberto* (1935), about the henpecked victim of three generations of women, also won prizes in both countries. The dramatist's native country tried to make amends by sending him as its consular representative to various countries, for he was becoming known as the Latin American dramatist whose name appeared most frequently on billboards around the world, but Moock, with his stubborn streak, would not come back to Chile. He died in Buenos Aires.

With the decreasing demand for Chilean nitrate, and the decline in value of the peso following the end of the First World War, the Chilean theater also declined. Then about 1940 began a renaissance. Two professional companies of actors were established, supported by the University of Chile and by the Catholic University in Santiago. And gradually a couple of dramatic schools also came into being.

They provided not only training for dramatists but development of actors, directors, stage designers, and even ballet dancers. Funds from the University of Chile supported the nation's National Symphony Orchestra.

One interesting result of this feverish Chilean interest in the theater was the entrance of women into a field previously dominated by men. As Carmen Laforet in Spain showed women that they could compete with masculine authors when she won the coveted Nadal Prize in 1944 with her novel *Nada* (Nothing), so women in Chile began realizing that there was a demand for their play manuscripts. Some of the feminine pioneer dramatists have been almost forgotten, except by researchers. They include "Delie Rouge" (Delia Rojas de White), who died of tuberculosis in 1943, Gaby von

Bussenius, and Luisa Zanelli López whose plays numb red thirty. Following their start, the fiction writer Madgalena Petit dramatized her historical novel *La Quintrala* (The Passion Flower, 1935), about a seventeenth-century Chilean murderess. The daughter and wife of Chilean diplomats, Ester Larraín Irarrázaval, who had come to know dram during official assignments abroad, wrote a number of plays under the pen name of "Gloria Morena." Finally came a quartet of women who wrote plays during time off from their regular activities and brought life and glory to the Chilean stage.

Dr. María Asunción Requena, a dentist by profession, won a number of prizes with her plays. Her first effort, *Míster Jones llega a las ocho* (Mr. Jones Arrives at Eight) won the 1952 National Theater Competition. Next came her *Fuerte Bulnes,* a historical play about a Chilean frontier town, that was given a prize in 1953, a performance in 1955, and a translation in Hungary in 1959. Later plays by her continued to receive awards, *El criadero de zorros en Magallanes* (The Foxherder of the Magellan Straits) about a woman ranch administrator in Tierra del Fuego who was forced to choose between her love for the land and love for a man. After a second play set in southern Chile, *Pan caliente* (Warm Bread), that was judged the best Chilean play of 1958, Dr. Requena chose another woman as protagonist of her *El camino más largo* (The Longest Road, 1959). This drama followed the long road traveled by Dr. Ernestina Pérez to become Chile's first woman physician.

Two other women in this "Generation of 1950" gain their livelihood from the theater: Isidora Aguirre who is professor in a School of Drama and Gabriela Roepke, director of drama in three or four Santiago schools. After completing several delightful short plays about women, much performed by amateur groups, Mrs. Aguirre wrote the libretto for a charming musical comedy, *La pérgola de las flores* (The Pergola of Flowers) which, after an exciting debut in Santiago in 1959 went on tour to Argentina and Europe. Among her dozen plays is one in collaboration with the Chilean novelist Manuel Rojas (1895—). It is a serious tragedy dealing with lower-class problems in what they call *Población Esperanza* (The Village of Hope, 1959), set in a suburb of Santiago. Miss Roepke's psychological plays have won prizes in Chile, served as samples of that nation's output in Peru, and appeared in translation in the United States where she received part of her theatrical training. At present she is teaching Spanish in the United States.

The fourth woman, Dinka Villarroel (1909—) born in Lota, southern Chile, is less well known though Acevedo Hernández recognized her ability and wrote a foreword for her first play, *Campamentos* (1945), that studied labor problems in the Chilean nitrate region. Mrs. Villarroel also dramatized the ignorant Araucanian Indians in their clashes with grasping white landowners. She has not written as many plays as her sister dramatists, but she has been active among the Chilean amateur groups that meet in annual drama competition.

Chilean men, too, have contributed to what has become one of Latin America's most active theatrical movements. Luis Alberto Heiremans (1928–64) was not only author of Chile's first important modern musical comedy *Esta señorita Trini* (This Miss Trinidad, 1958), but also of a series of dramatic successes. His three-act *La jaula en el árbol* (The Cage in the Tree) not only won the Critics Award for 1957, but was performed in Chicago and in Bristol, England. His plays are noteworthy for their human sympathy and spiritual force. His death of cancer at the age of 36 was a great loss to the theater.

From the many other male contributors to Chile's theater it is hard to make a selection. Sergio Vodánocic (1926—) was a success from his first attempt, *El senador no es honorable* (The Senator is not Honorable, 1951). His *Mi mujer necesita marido* (My Wife Needs a Husband, 1953) was made into a successful movie in Mexico. After he had studied drama in the United States, his *Deja que los perros ladren* (Let the Dogs Bark, 1958), about a father willing to do anything to become rich and his idealistic son who started to imitate him, won the 1960 Municipal Prize, was performed in Argentina, Spain, and the United States, and also appeared as a movie.

Egon Raúl Wolff (1926—), an English-trained chemical engineer by profession, writes powerful plays of social criticism. He began with *Discípulos de miedo* (Followers of Fear, 1957) and *Mansión de lechuza* (Owl House, 1958) both of which had their first draft in English. His satire on Chile's upper crust, *Parejas de trapo* (Rag Couples) won a 1960 competition where it was called a well-constructed play with powerful characterization. *La niña madre* (1960), also called "La Polla," and in its English translation at Yale University "A Touch of Blue," is considered his masterpiece, and one of the best plays of Chile's current theater. More recently he wrote *Las 49 estrellas* (The 49 Stars) and *Los invasores* (The Invaders), with its chief character an industrialist who dreams his possessions are seized from him by beggars, helped by his son.

Another developing psychological playwright is Alejandro Sieveking (1935—) who might be called one of the "beat generation" of angry young men. *La madre de los conejos* (The Rabbits' Mother, 1961) was well received and *Parecido a la felicidad* (Resembling Happiness, 1959) was taken on a tour of ten Latin American nations by a troupe of drama school graduates. It has something of the flavor of Tennessee Williams.

Most of these dramatists wrote for the two university groups already mentioned. One group started as the Experimental Theater of the National University of Chile about 1940. The other, connected with the Catholic University, came into being in 1943 as el Teatro de Ensayo with about the same meaning. The first eventually became ITUCH and

the second TEUC. Most of their productions are serious
works. For humor one must look to the commercial theaters,
many of them small and frequently located in basements.

One of Chile's most active professional theaters is
headed by Manuel Frank (1920—), who began offering
translations of sophisticated foreign plays. Finally he decided
he could save royalties and have greater appeal and larger
audiences if he wrote his own offerings. *Tempo de vals*
(Waltz Time, 1952) proved he was right. It was followed by
Punto muerto (Dead Center), suggested perhaps, as the
dramatist said, by *Blithe Spirit,* but far from a slavish imita-
tion. Actually it is a psychological melodrama with only
three characters. *Matrimonio para tres* (Marriage for Three)
his comedy for 1955, introduces a woman who needs a baby
to claim a wealthy estate. Since her husband was apparently
killed in an airplane accident, she takes up with another
man. The return of her husband poses a problem in pater-
nity. In 1958 came *El hombre del siglo* (The Man of the Century), translated in this volume.

I saw my first Frank play performed one rainy Sunday
night in Santiago. Since the seating capacity of the theater
was so small, I could not be assured of a ticket, but on that
possibility, I waited around and finally just before curtain
time was ushered to a seat. It was a chummy audience, everybody talking to everybody, and most of them apparently ac-
quainted with Frank's previous plays. "Oh, you'll enjoy it,"
was the unsought assurance of my neighbor. And he was
right. I was fortunate enough to see two other plays presented by Frank's company while in Santiago. *The Man of
the Century* seemed to me the one with most appeal to North
American audiences, though in a letter to me its author com-
mented that he thought a more serious play, like perhaps *La
primera piedra* (The First Stone), might be more rewarding.
This latter follows the Scriptural admonition about the person to cast the first stone.

Other plays by him include the comedy *La terrible Caro-*

lina (1954), *El amigo de la casa* (The Friend of the Family, 1955) and others that provoke both laughter and thought. *Duérmete, Gabriela* (Go to Sleep, Gabriela) was finished in 1965.

As I worked word by word and sentence by sentence translating *The Man of the Century*, I realized something I had not observed during the performance—the theatrical skill of the dramatist. The dialogue seems so inevitable, and all possible value is squeezed from each scene. Those who may be somewhat startled by a Chilean's fifty-million-peso business deal should realize that the Chilean peso began dropping in buying power following the end of the First World War as Chilean salitre was replaced by the cheaper synthetic Swedish nitrate extracted from the air. In 1960, when the peso had dropped to 1,000 to $1.00 that unit was replaced by the escudo with an assigned value of $1.00, though in 1969 it had depreciated to nearly 9 to a dollar. So, whether fifty million pesos really represents a breath-taking business deal or not depends on the period covered by the play. However, the fun, satire, and suspense of the comedy have little relationship to the sum involved. Certainly the contract meant much to the business man, and was abundant cause for worry, with a cocktail party coming up and no servants, in a country where a houseful of servants was taken for granted.

This is Frank's first play to be translated into English and is one of the few long Chilean plays to have appeared in English.

Argentina

THIRD OF THE NATIONS represented in this volume is Argentina, which for a long time enjoyed the greatest theatrical activity in Spanish America. Even today it has more commercial theaters functioning than any other nation. Many volumes have been written about its dramatists and their plays.

Sharing the River Plate as boundary with Uruguay, Argentina and its neighbor have developed together, sharing playwrights and actors. Traces of a dawning theater have been discovered in Argentina as early as 1717, but the first performances to be described in detail celebrated the coronation of Ferdinand VI in 1747, when a quartet of Golden Age dramas, performed in the main plaza on a temporary stage, entertained as many of Buenos Aires' 10,223 inhabitants as could crowd around. To understand its slow growth, one must remember that Mexico and the Pacific Coast were colonized long before anyone was interested in territory along Southern Atlantic waters where there were neither deposits of valuable metals nor large populations of Indians to be of use to Spaniards.

The rise in status of the River Plate region to a Viceregency in 1776 and the arrival of its first viceroy in 1778 gave the first real impetus to drama. Viceroy Vertiz wanted his dominion to be culturally equal to anything in the New World, so he encouraged the erection of La Ranchería Theater, where plays began at 7 P.M. in summer and 6 P.M. in winter. Everybody was urged to attend. When some of the wealthy citizens complained about dark streets for their homeward trip after a show, the Viceroy decreed a system of street lighting, the first in the New World.

For lack of manuscripts from Madrid, a call was made on local writers. One to respond was José Lavardén (1754–1810). He composed *Siropo,* a tragedy about the wife of one of Sebastian Cabot's companions on the voyage of discovery to the Río de la Plata. She spurned the love of an Indian chief even though it meant her husband's torture and her own death by burning. This first version of a story that became popular among Argentine writers was performed at the Ranchería on Carnival Sunday, 1789.

La Ranchería shortly afterward suffered the fate of so

many wooden Latin American theaters, set ablaze by some of
its footlights. But other theaters with other plays soon replaced it in this developing port. In addition to many products of Spain, there were several locally written that deserve
to be noted: *El amor de la estanciera* (The Love of the
Ranch Girl, 1787?) whose author has never been definitely
identified, and *Las bodas de Chivico and Pancha* (The Marriage of Chivico and Fanny, 1823), with its authentic gauchos and their home in the pampas.

After another century of plays of all kinds, largely from
Spain or influenced by Spanish models, came the work of Argentina's first national dramatist, the Salesian priest Nemisio
Trejo (1862–1916), author of hits with such topical titles as
La visita del gaucho (The Gaucho's Visit) and *Un día en la
capital* (A Day in the Capital, 1890). One of them, *El
político* (The Politician), set a record with five hundred
performances. Many presented the local cowboy, or gaucho.

And it was gaucho plays that started the contemporary
River Plate theater on its successful course. One of the popular forms of entertainment in Buenos Aires was the circus,
whose acrobatic and animal-taming acts usually ended in
some wild pantomime, under such titles as *The Italian Bandits of Calabria.* They included shooting and displays of
horsemanship. However, to end its 1884 season in Buenos
Aires, the Carlo Brothers North American Circus wanted
something more national. So they commissioned the novelist
Eduardo Gutiérrez (1853–90) to make a pantomime from
his serial novel *Juan Moreira,* an idealized story of a gaucho
oppressed by the law. Actually he had been an ugly, treacher-
ous criminal.

It showed the gaucho trying to recover money lent to an
Italian storekeeper, only to be denied by the judge. In his
anger, the thwarted Juan stabbed the Italian, tried to flee,
and was stabbed in the back by soldiers. With that pantomime, the circus concluded its season, and moved on to Brazil.

The next year when the circus returned to Argentina for another season, it was suggested that for the finale, dialogue be added. Since the original novelist was more interested in his current project, the Uruguayan clown José Podestá, who had been taking the part of Juan Moreira because he could play the guitar and sing, supplied the conversation with the help of the novel. The result was the popularization on the stage of the wronged gaucho, a character who had appeared earlier chiefly in fiction and poetry.

Of the gaucho theme, as with the cowboy in the western United States, only a limited number of variations is possible. He can have run-ins with the law; he can join the law and use cowboy tactics to achieve justice; he can be a Jewish cowboy; he can look like Jesus of Nazareth and argue for peace but resort to violence and end chained between two thieving cowboys, like the García Veloso character in 1902. There can be female gauchos, but eventually writers of gaucho plays begin repeating themselves. Finally with Alberto Vacarezza (1888–1859), born three years after the first gaucho play and himself author of several of the better examples, the movement came to an end. He wrote its epitaph in his comedy *El cantar del gaucho* (The Gaucho Song, 1950), for the San Martín centenary.

Meanwhile another character had come to take his place on the stage. In later performances of *Juan Moreira,* an Italian called Cocoliche and speaking barbarous Spanish had been inserted to provide comedy. Gradually this gringo became a popular figure, representative of the large number of immigrants pouring into Argentina. No one knows for a certainty the origin of that word "gringo." Some think it a distortion of "griego" (Greek), whose speech was "all Greek" to the native Argentine. Sometimes it was used to cover all the foreigners flocking to Argentina; sometimes it referred only to the Italians, who made up the greater number of the newcomers. Certainly "gringo" is not derived, as is sometimes stated, from the song of the Texas cowboy, "Green grow the rushes, O!" The term appeared in South America long before they had heard of American cowboys along the Río Grande.

But whatever its source, dramatists introduced the gringo in all aspects and stages of his amalgamation into River Plate life—aboard the ships, entering the country, trying to make a living, and finally as the industrious laborer in competition with the casual creole, or Argentine-born Spaniard. It was not long before he began taking over farms and property of the easy-going Argentines. By the act he passed from a comic character to a serious threat to those who had been living without effort on the Argentine pampas. Serious dramas about the gringo and his impact on the local economy, by playwrights like Martín Coronado (1850–1919) and Roberto Payró (1867–1928), preceded the appearance of the River Plate dramatist best known abroad, Florencio Sánchez (1875–1910).

Born in Montevideo, Uruguay, one of eleven children of itinerant parents, Sánchez got his education on the street among the poor people. He first attracted attention on account of a play written in a couple of days, *M'hijo el dotor* (My Son the Lawyer, 1903). It embodies most of the flaws found in his later plays: a scatter-shot attack on too many injustices and evil social conditions, unconvincing psychology and logic, and unnatural conversation by the upper class with whom he had never associated. But it also revealed his ability to provide excellent theater, convincing lower-class speech, and an interesting story.

Following this play came nineteen more, seven full length and twelve short, the product of the six years of Sánchez's career as a dramatist. *La gringa* (The Foreign Girl, 1904) is supposed to have taken him only a day to set down on the back of telegraph blanks which in his poverty he used as paper. Actually he had thought about it and lived it for several years. It is somewhat misnamed because the main character is rather the inefficient creole Cantalicio than Victoria the daughter of Italian immigrants. But it and *Ba-*

rranca abajo (Down the Gully, 1905) are the best rounded out of all his work, authentic pictures of the lower-class dwellers in the pampas. Critics still argue which is the better of these two rural plays. Only in the second one, however, in his portrayal of the good gaucho Zoilo, driven to despair by his womenfolk, does Sánchez offer a complete personality. In his later plays set in the city, ignorance of the ways of the upper classes which he describes and his attempts to uphold unconvincing theses, weaken their impact. He is more successful in presenting living people in his shorter plays.

At his death, Florencio Sánchez had established no school. He left no one who might be called his successor. After his time, dramatists branched out in all directions, and there were so many of them that Tito Livio Foppa needed a thick volume for his *Diccionario teatral del Río de la Plata* (1962). Obviously it is impossible to refer to them all here, though I am sure their admirers will criticize me for the dramatists I fail to mention.

Certainly Gregorio de Laferrère (1867–1913) should be included. As Sánchez developed the tragic theater, so Laferrère founded the cosmopolitan comedy. *Jettatore* (1904) tells of a man supposedly able to turn his evil eye on his enemies and jinx them. His *Las de Barranco* (The Barranco Women, 1908) is probably the best example of this dramatist's capability, with its remarkable fourth act conversation and pathetic curtain.

Pedro Pico (1882–1945) was the outstanding Argentine dramatist of the early twentieth century, always trusted to provide entertainment, though sometimes at the expense of logic and veracity. He is one of the few early Argentine dramatists who made a living by his pen. He dramatized the social problems of the immigrants and wrote several realistic plays about life and tribulations on the pampas, but he was especially known as an interpreter of women, in plays like *Las rayas de una cruz* (Rays from a Cross, 1940).

Armando Discépolo (1887–1952) brought the influence

of Pirandello and other Europeans to the River Plate stage
by translating and directing many foreign plays. He is remembered as the inventor of the "grotesco criollo," about
nonconformists, whose tragic flaw is their inability to change
with the changing times. A good example is *Stéfano* (1928)
about a musician who attributes to his associates the causes
of his own failure, or *Mateo* (1923) who expects his horse
and cab to earn him a living after the arrival of the automobile.

Of this period, the dramatist picked for immortality and
often named as one of the three greatest of the Spanish
American world, was the Russian Jew, Samuel Eichelbaum
(1894—). Beginning first as a collaborator of Pedro Pico,
he found his own initial style in the Ibsenian tragedy *La
mala sed* (Evil Thirst, 1920), a play of the conscious and the
unconscious in which the father's dominating sex urge is
transmitted to his son and to his daughter. After other violent and melodramatic plays, in 1929 Eichelbaum wrote
Cuando tengas un hijo (When You Have a Son) about a father, his lonely son groping for understanding, and a lonely
woman. A North American critic called it "One of the most
moving, heartbreaking, simple, unassuming, real plays ever
written."—Theodore Apstein, "Samuel Eichelbaum, Argentine Playwright," *Books Abroad* 19 (1945), 237.

About 1938, after having written other plays, Eichelbaum entered his mature period with more credible characters and with external action added to his early philoso-
phizing. One example is *Un guapo del 900* (A Twentieth-
Century Bully, 1940), about the two bodyguards of a politician and their wine-swizzling mother Natividad. As with
so many of his plays, Eichelbaum offers no solution nor indicates the outcome. He states the problem and leaves its
answer up to the reader or audience.

A dramatist easier to read and one who sends his audiences away in a less troubled state of mind is Conrado Nalé
Roxlo (1898—), who began his literary career as writer of

humorous verse. At the age of forty-two he began combining humor and fantasy in his first stage play, *La cola de la sirena* (The Mermaid's Tail), then four years later came a comedy set in Argentina's colonial period. *Una viuda difícil* (A Difficult Widow) tells the story of a seven-time murderer whom the Viceroy will release on his birthday if some one will marry him. The widow Isabel is ripe to sacrifice herself, only to find that the "murderer" is a timid man who had claimed the crimes to give himself status.

Nalé Roxlo followed this success with several others, always varying his theme and treatment. *El pacto de Cristina* (Christine's Pact) is a personalized inversion of the Faust theme. *Judith y las rosas* (1956) is built around a bible story.

Argentine stages were also filled by plays written in collaboration. Practically all the early dramatists combined with someone else for a play or two. Pico had at least eight associates at various times. Few of the partners remained together very long, but two who never wrote individually and who were among the most successful of these *binomios* or collaborators are Juan Fernando Camilo Darthés (1889—) a business man, and Dr. Carlos S. Damel (1890–1959), an eye surgeon.

First of the fifty plays they wrote together was the brief *La última escena* (The Final Scene, 1911) in which the protagonist kills his sweetheart with a hatpin! It was completed while the two were still in the university, and ran for four performances. In their subsequent endeavors, they were rewarded by longer runs. Their final collaboration, the comedy *Envidia* (Envy), was in its hundredth showing the night that Dr. Damel died. When I once asked about their method of working together, Señor Darthés sent a reply which I translate:

"We wrote our comedies by discussing them, a serious discussion. Of course we argued in good faith with a desire to convince the other one. That was the only way we knew to convince an audience. As for the technique, nothing could be simpler. Our point of departure was an idea embodied in a character. That determined the basic, central situation. When we had come to an agreement on these three points, idea, character, and situation, we discussed the complications and ramifications which in their turn determined the other characters. The dialog, the plot, and the conclusion came out as the development went on, which we almost always handled aloud. When that was thoroughly discussed and completed, came the easiest part, writing the play. Damel usually dictated and Darthés typed it out. Of course after the writing we faced the correcting and polishing, to make everything clear and definite, since the first version was often verbose. But matters of syntax are mechanical. The real creative work came during our arguments. I don't dare declare that light came from the discussions, but I do affirm, from experience, that our successes as well as our failures in the theatre came from them."

Latin Americans speak slightingly of "The Buenos Aires Play," a light, humorous, sure-fire hit with amusing dialogue, some slight attempt at characterization, and a happy ending, but brittle and built on a formula. During the height of theatrical activity in Buenos Aires, the professional theaters were full of this sort of production. Some of the Darthés-Damel collaborations fall into this category, but they were never worried whether they were writing great art or not. If they provided their audiences with pleasure and entertainment, they were willing to leave art to Calderón, Shakespeare, or Ibsen.

But some of their plays departed considerably from the Buenos Aires play formula. One was their favorite, *Los chicos crecen* (The Children Grow Up, 1937), winner of a National drama prize that has brought the collaborators royalties from more than four thousand performances all over the Spanish-speaking world. Its chief character is the failure, Cazanave who came to Buenos Aires and was befriended by Dr. Zapiola. At a time when Cazanave was thought to be mortally ill, the doctor to protect his reputation borrowed his friend's name under which to register the children of the doctor and his mistress. By this act he made her Cazanave's common-law wife. Beginning with this situation, all sorts of complications follow before the final satisfying conclusion.

During our correspondence about including a translation of *La hermana Josefina* in this anthology, Señor Darthés sent me a recent revision of *Los chicos crecen* which he considers of greater universal interest and higher literary value than Josefina, which he calls "light and of less importance (*transcendencia*)." However that other play brought up the question for which I have never received a complete answer from any River Plate dramatist to whom I have put it. If the theater mirrors everyday life, does the vast number of comedies presenting illegitimate children mean that there is more infidelity in Argentina than in other parts of the world? The only reply I ever got was: "They make a good subject for comedy."

However, for my purpose, to give idea of the customs of other people through their plays, *La hermana Josefina* is a better choice. Its employment, for instance, of the River Plate word "curandera" points up the use of practical nurses in lands where doctors are scarce. The Chileans call them "meicas," derived from the feminine form of "médico" doctor, but with the "d" lacking, and those quack doctors or witch doctors covered by the term also have something lacking, a medical training. "The Long Road," written by the Chilean dramatist María Asunción Requena concerns the long, hard road that had to be followed by any Latin American woman ambitious to become a physician. And *La hermana Josefina* goes even farther, since after getting her diploma, she still faces the problem of finding patients. A reader can realize how low the status of women used to be.

Most of the Darthés-Damel plays are set in Buenos Aires, where the two collaborators spent their lives. Of them, the dean of Argentine theatrical criticism, Arturo Beringuer Ca-

risomo, said in his Introduction to *Teatro Argentino* (1962):
"I do not hestiate to affirm that, with the passing of years,
when we are interested in knowing how Buenos Aires was in
their time, before the 1943 revolution and the 1945 social
changes, the comedies of Darthés and Damel will be a testi-
mony of precious national quality. Theirs is Argentine theatre in the best sense of the phrase." *La hermana Josefina,*
which is set in a small town south of the capital, is an exception, but it does display a combination of universality and
local color, with its minute observation of the world, and all
in a sentimental vein. Its original run in 1938 was 114 performances, with frequent revivals. The comedy proves that if
the Spanish Alvarez Quinteros have spiritual brothers in the
New World, here they are.

Willis Knapp Jones

Miami University
Oxford, Ohio
September 18, 1969

MEN
and ANGELS

Three South American Comedies

The Quack Doctor

A COMEDY IN THREE ACTS

CHARACTERS

Sister Josephine,
the quack doctor
Manuel Ordóñez,
her assistant
First Patient
Second Patient
Doctor Zubiaga,
a legitimate doctor
The Gringo (*Italian*)

His Wife
The Mother
The Father
First Detective
Second Detective
Chief Investigator
A Local Policeman,
who does not speak

ACT 1
Scene 1

*The office of the Quack Doctor. A writing table consid-
erably worn. Chairs and benches of various styles and ages.
On a pillar in a corner, a skull. On a table, a fishbowl in
which swim several goldfish. A number of books. An hour-
glass. A switchboard with buttons, labels, and light switches.
Hanging on the wall a bottle with am embalmed poison
snake. Upstage left, toward the corner, a large window. Upstage right, a door to the waiting room.*

*As the curtain rises, Manuel sits at the desk. He is a man
of about fifty, wearing a gaucho blouse, baggy gaucho trousers, slippers, and a yellow handkerchief around his neck. He
is talking over the phone.*

MANUEL: Hello! No, not today. What about tomorrow? Appointment number 32. No, she has nothing open before
that. Tell her to come for that. Goodbye. (*He hangs up,
thinks a minute, then takes off the receiver and pushes a
button.*) Hey, Pancho, take over the calls, will you till I
tell you? (*Hangs up. Enter Sister Josephine, very well
dressed. She is no more than 32. She is very pretty, small,
but energetic; intelligent, but easygoing.*)
JOSEPHINE (*tossing her hat onto the desk*):   Good morning,
Manuel.
MANUEL: Good morning, Miss Josephine. You must have
got up early today.
JOSEPHINE: Yes, I've just come from Tres Arroyos.
MANUEL: Did you send the money?

4

JOSEPHINE: Yes, four thousand five hundred.

MANUEL: Four thousand five hundred pesos in twenty days. At that rate, we'll end the month with seven thousand pesos.

JOSEPHINE: It was about time. After all our sacrifices. Have you ever thought, Manuel, about what we've had to do to earn this?

MANUEL: It doesn't keep me awake nights any more.

JOSEPHINE: Yes, after all, who can deny that we're really doing some good?

MANUEL: That's true. Three came yesterday from Buenos Aires on the night train. They're staying at the Hotel International.

JOSEPHINE: How hard it's going to be to give up all this! There must be fifty patients out there waiting. Have you looked at any of them?

MANUEL: No, not looked at them. I've spent my time listening, but there are so many that it's hard to pick out who's talking.

JOSEPHINE: Well, let's listen. Turn it on, will you? (*Manuel goes to the desk and pushes a button. A conversation can be heard over the loud speaker.*)

FIRST PATIENT: She was right about me, all right. I took the second bath in the beaver pond Tuesday night when the moon was full, and every one of my pimples disappeared.

SECOND PATIENT (*in a very provincial dialect*):   You don't say! I know everybody is talking about her. That's why I came so far to see her. I live fifty miles away, beyond Ghost Gully, near the ranch of Oligario, him that died last month.

FIRST: What's your trouble?

SECOND: It's not me. It's my wife.

FIRST: And where did you leave her? At the inn?

SECOND: No, I didn't bring her along.

FIRST: How do you expect Sister Josephine to cure her?

SECOND: I brought along one of her stockings, because the pain is in her leg. She broke it, understand? She walks with her toes pointing straight up. It's her heel, poor woman.

(Josephine makes a gesture to Manuel to turn off the loud speaker. He obeys by punching a button.)

JOSEPHINE: Have them come in.

(Manuel opens the door of the vestibule, where several patients try to push in. A confusion of voices can be heard.)

MANUEL *(in a voice of authority)*: Take it easy! Don't push! Don't push! She'll see you all if you'll just have patience. Now then, numbers one and two. Come in.

(Enter the two who were heard talking over the loud speaker. Manuel closes the door. Josephine looks at the First Patient.)

JOSEPHINE: Well, did you bring the hens?

FIRST: Yes, Sister. I left them in the kitchen, all four of them.

JOSEPHINE *(changing her tone of voice)*: Four! What am I going to do with four? I told you eight, one for each joint that's rheumatic. Are they white hens?

FIRST: Well, a little mixed, but almost white.

JOSEPHINE: I told you white hens and big enough to cover the joints. You know I have to open them, take out the insides, mix the liver with ashes and willow leaves, and chop everything up with the wing feathers. That's what is used on the parts that hurt. And afterward the opened hen is laid on to extract the sickness. It must suck, suck, two, three, four days. And on the fifth, the swelling of the joints will go down and be cured, and the pain will be gone. So get out of here and don't come back without eight fat, white hens.

FIRST: Very well. I'll try to bring them tomorrow.

JOSEPHINE *(taking several papers from a box)* :   Until you're back with the hens, take one of these every night. There are five. Then come and see me again.

FIRST *(reaching into his pocket)* :   How much do I owe you?

JOSEPHINE: We'll discuss that later when you're cured. *(as the patient turns toward the door)* Listen here! Who are you voting for?

FIRST: Why . . . I . . . uh, I don't know. For anyone they tell me to.

JOSEPHINE: Then remember. I'm the one that does the telling around here. Before you vote, come and see me. And bring all your friends, even those who aren't sick.

FIRST: Very well, Sister. Goodbye. *(Again he starts away.)*

MANUEL: Oh, and say Hello to Pelaia, as you go by. Tell him the last cheeses he sent me were very good but we've eaten them all and we haven't any left.

FIRST: Yes, Don Manuel. *(Exit.)*

JOSEPHINE *(staring at the Second Patient)* :   Well, what about you?

SECOND: Here I am. I've traveled fifty miles to get your help.

JOSEPHINE: Where have I seen you? Where have I seen you? *(Silence. Manuel switches on a red light. Pondering, Josephine sits on the corner of the desk. She looks at the fish in the fishbowl that is now illuminated by the red light, as if it were a reflector.)*

MANUEL *(to the Second Patient, who gets up surprised)* :   Don't talk! Let her concentrate. *(muttering an incantation)* Ayapurá Mamboecopé! Help her, good spirits. Enter into her body. Illuminate her thoughts, give light to her eyes, so that they may pierce through light and shadow, and look into the soul! *(He makes several strange gestures.)*

JOSEPHINE: Not long ago, either. Oh, yes, now I remember. *(She closes her eyes and raises her head.)* I saw you walking with your sick wife. I saw you holding her arm so she wouldn't fall. She was walking with the tip of her foot pointing straight up. Walking on her heel, poor woman! It was far from here. Beyond Ghost Gully, near the ranch of Oligario, who died not long ago.

SECOND: That's where we live.

JOSEPHINE: Very well. Show me the stocking you brought me.

SECOND (*holding up the paper in which he had wrapped the stocking*): She's a witch! She knows everything.

MANUEL: Of course she does. She is very powerful. But hush. Let her concentrate. (*She has taken the package, pulled out the stocking, laid it across the fishbowl, and looks at it for a moment in silence.*)

JOSEPHINE: Hard, very hard! The bones have been set wrong. And not much lime. They're joined in a curve. The way they were set. Don't you see? Look here! The shin bone is out of place. There! The poor woman!

SECOND: I don't see anything.

MANUEL: How could you? You don't have X-ray in your eyes like her. Hush! Let her speak.

JOSEPHINE: Hard! This is no job for me. Why should I deceive you? If you had brought her to me two weeks ago, when the break was fresh . . . But now, no! Turn the light on, Manuel. (*He turns it on and extinguishes the red light. Josephine rolls up the stocking. She drops into a chair with her face in her hands. The Second Patient takes a step toward her.*)

MANUEL: No! (*stopping her*) Let her rest. That is hard work. Whenever she concentrates, this always happens. But don't worry.

SECOND: So you think there's nothing can be done, do you?

MANUEL: Oh, there's something can be done. But this calls for an operation. She doesn't handle that sort of work.

SECOND: Do I owe her something?

JOSEPHINE: No, nothing. You may leave. (*as he reaches the door*) Tell me, whom are you voting for?

SECOND: At home we always vote with the government.

JOSEPHINE: That's fine, then. I'll call you when I need you. (*Exit the Second Patient. For some time a white bulb has been blinking on the desk.*) Look! Someone's on the phone. (*From now on, the two resume their ordinary way of talking, as at the beginning of the act.*)

MANUEL (*picking up the receiver*):   What is it, Pancho? Who? What doctor? Zubiaga? (*Josephine goes toward the phone.*) The doctor? (*covering the mouthpiece with his hand*) Dr. Zubiaga wants to know if you'll see him.

JOSEPHINE: Here! Give me it! (*over the phone*) Pancho, put him on. (*to Manuel*) This is marvelous! (*on the phone*) Hello. Hello who is it? Oh, yes, doctor. Speaking! It's a pleasure. Is it you who are ill? No? What a pity! (*She laughs.*) No I just said that because here we are specialists in treating the sick. (*She laughs.*) Oh, no! Why should I make you wait when you are practically a colleague? (*Laughs.*) Patients? Oh, yes, there are a number in the waiting room. All those people you don't cure. But aren't you afraid you'll be seen? Why, because it might damage your reputation. A real doctor visiting a quack doctor. Just imagine! Aren't you afraid? Very well. Where are you? In the outer office? I'll call, myself, and tell them to let you in. Yes, I'll see you at once. (*Hangs up.*)

MANUEL: What? Do you mean you are going to see him?

JOSEPHINE: Why not?

MANUEL: Be careful! Who knows what trouble he's bringing?

JOSEPHINE: I'm dying of curiosity to see what *does* bring him here. I'll go and fix up a bit. Have him shown in here. (*Exit Josephine rapidly, left. Manuel rearranges several chairs. Then he goes to the door, right, and opens it. Enter Dr. Zubiaga. He takes off his hat.*)

MANUEL: Come in, doctor.

ZUBIAGA: Good morning, sir. (*He is a man of about 30, at-*

*tractive, well dressed, but somewhat affected, and mark-
edly ironical in speaking.*)

MANUEL: Good morning, doctor.

ZUBIAGA: Has the uh . . . the doctor gone out?

MANUEL: Sister Josephine will be here in a minute. May I
take your hat?

ZUBIAGA: No, thank you. I'm staying only a minute. (*pause*)
Are you very busy?

MANUEL: Indeed we are, doctor.

ZUBIAGA (*who from the instant he entered has been observing the contents of the room*) :   It looks that way. You
seem to get a lot of patients. Is that a yacaré snake?

MANUEL: Yes, doctor. We use its oil.

ZUBIAGA (*smiling*) :   For your automobile?

MANUEL: To cure sores and bruises, doctor. It's an excellent
remedy for all skin diseases.

ZUBIAGA (*pointing to the goldfish in the bowl*) :   What do
you do with those?

MANUEL: With those we cure the ills of the soul.

ZUBIAGA: Do you serve them fried to the suffers?

MANUEL: You laugh, doctor, because you don't understand.
Occultism, like medicine, is a science. Those little fish
have brought tranquility to many a soul.

ZUBIAGA: Those goldfish? Oh, of course! You rely on faith.

MANUEL: Here is Sister Josephine, doctor. With your permission, I'll leave. (*Exit Manuel, right, just as Josephine
comes in, left. Zubiaga stares at her in stupefaction.*)

JOSEPHINE: Good morning, Doctor Zubiaga. It's a pleasure
to meet you. What's the matter? You seem surprised.

ZUBIAGA: Indeed, I am. I can't get over it. Are you really
Sister Josephine?

JOSEPHINE (*extending her hand*) :   Sister Josephine in body
and soul.

ZUBIAGA (*shaking her hand*) :   It's my pleasure. But I imag-
ined you were some sort of elderly monkey.

JOSEPHINE: Monkey, perhaps, but hardly elderly. I assure you I am not something from before Christ.

ZUBIAGA: How miserably have I been deceived! Neither monkey nor elderly. You're an enchanting woman!

JOSEPHINE: Oh, doctor! But let me take your hat, and please sit down.

ZUBIAGA: Thank you, but I mustn't stay long. You have many patients waiting.

JOSEPHINE: Oh, don't worry about them. My patients are accustomed to waiting.

ZUBIAGA (*still standing and with his hat in his hand*) :   This is why I am here. I have a patient. Well along in years, you know. Don Indalecio Rosales. The owner of the power plant. I don't know whether you know him. (*Josephine shakes her head.*) Well, he's critically ill. Unfortunately nothing can be done for him.

JOSEPHINE: What a pity!

ZUBIAGA: He can't last more than a couple of weeks. I've told the family the truth, quite frankly, but you know how people are. They've heard about your miraculous cures. Yesterday his wife and two daughters expressed the desire to have you called in as a last resort. Well, I . . . frankly . . .

JOSEPHINE: You objected.

ZUBIAGA: At first, yes. Why deny it? But after thinking it over . . . Since science has exhausted its resources . . . Well, any way, they were so insistent that last night I gave in. After all, it's natural to give in to people when there's nothing else to do. So you see . . . Well, here I am to ask you to come and look at him.

JOSEPHINE: From what is he suffering?

ZUBIAGA (*purposely trying to overawe her*) :   Apparently it is a neoplasm of the stomach with metathesis to the liver, a hypertrophic liver that can be palpated and extends four finger breadths below the umbilical line.

JOSEPHINE: You needn't go on, doctor. Is he quite thin?

ZUBIAGA: He's in a cachetic state.

JOSEPHINE (*smiling*): You confuse me, doctor, with the terms you use. If you had said his liver was large or small, or if he had diphtheria or not, we'd understand each other better, I'm a layman. You aren't very considerate of me.

ZUBIAGA: Excuse me! You're right. Just a matter of habit. I forgot I wasn't talking to a colleague. Well, in a word, he has a dangerous tumor. It's cancer.

JOSEPHINE: That's what you think?

ZUBIAGA: Not "think." I'm sure.

JOSEPHINE: Doctors so often make mistakes. Why can't this be just one more?

ZUBIAGA: Believe me, this is no time to use charms or amulets.

JOSEPHINE: Who knows? Don't jump to conclusions. I have saved so many hopeless cases.

ZUBIAGA: Then you'll go and look at him?

JOSEPHINE: Why not? This very afternoon. As soon as I've looked after my patients. There's no use telling you the hour, because of course you won't want to be there with me.

ZUBIAGA: Why not? Even if this isn't exactly a consultation of doctors, I'm a friend of the family. At what time do you want me to come for you in my car?

JOSEPHINE: No, doctor. That's too much bother. There will be no need for that. Besides, don't you have office hours this afternoon?

ZUBIAGA: Yes, but unfortunately I haven't as many patients as you have.

JOSEPHINE: Please sit down. Give me your hat. (*He obeys, mechanically.*) This isn't an office call. There'll be no charge. May I offer you something to drink? My own invention. I can mix it in an instant. (*She hangs up his hat.*)

ZUBIAGA (*as Josephine goes to a cabinet and takes out two glasses, three bottles, and a cocktail shaker*) : You're very kind. To see you in action. How could I refuse such a temptation?

JOSEPHINE: Have you been practicing long, doctor?

ZUBIAGA: Four years.

JOSEPHINE: You got your diploma in 1933?

ZUBIAGA: Yes, in 1933.

JOSEPHINE (*agitating the shaker*) : I had a young friend who graduated in 1933. Alberto Iparraguirre. Did you know him?

ZUBIAGA: The Basque? Of course! He and I interned together.

JOSEPHINE: Has he set up in practice?

ZUBIAGA: Yes, I think in Coronel Suárez.

JOSEPHINE: Doing all right?

ZUBIAGA: I don't know. At least struggling. That's what we are all doing.

JOSEPHINE (*handing him a glass*) : Here you are! I don't know whether you'll like it.

ZUBIAGA (*accepting the glass*) : Thank you.

JOSEPHINE: Here's to your success, doctor.

ZUBIAGA: I'm sorry I can't give you the same toast.

JOSEPHINE: Why not, doctor?

ZUBIAGA: Success came to you sometime ago. (*Drinks.*)

JOSEPHINE: So they say. Well, how do you like it?

ZUBIAGA: Delicious! I've never tasted anything like it.

JOSEPHINE: Vermouth, Olton Gin, and bitter orange. It's easy to make.

ZUBIAGA: Perhaps it needs the touch of your hands in mixing the ingredients.

JOSEPHINE: They're at your service if you need them.

ZUBIAGA (*offering her a cigaret*) : Do you smoke?

JOSEPHINE: Light tobacco, doctor?

ZUBIAGA: No, dark.

JOSEPHINE: Then I'm afraid I'll have to refuse. I prefer

light tobacco. (*She takes a wooden box out of the desk.*)
I get these from Buenos Aires. They have a pleasant
taste. Won't you try one?

ZUBIAGA (*taking one*) :   Thank you.

(*Josephine puts her cigaret in a long holder that she has
taken from a case. Zubiaga hurries to take a box of
matches from his pocket. He gets out a match and is
about to strike it. Meanwhile she has taken a lighter
from the desk and lights it first.*)

JOSEPHINE: Oh, doctor, do you still use old-fashioned
matches?

ZUBIAGA (*putting the box back into his pocket*) :   You're
right.

JOSEPHINE: May I light yours, doctor?

ZUBIAGA (*accepting the light and looking meanwhile into
her eyes*) :   I hadn't noticed. You have extraordinary
eyes. Sad, tragic. I can't decide exactly what color they
are.

JOSEPHINE: Like muscatel grapes, doctor.

ZUBIAGA: You must have consulted a color specialist.

JOSEPHINE: Quite true, a Galician clerk in the San Juan
store.

ZUBIAGA (*smiling*) :   Good. (*pause, then after a second
puff*) Fine! Uh . . . Have you been long in this . . . this,
what shall I call it?

JOSEPHINE: I call it a profession. A profession like any
other. I entered it because I had to.

ZUBIAGA: You can't complain. Things seem to be going
well for you.

JOSEPHINE: Fairly well. If it weren't for this life of terrible
sacrifice.

ZUBIAGA: Did you say sacrifice?

JOSEPHINE: Yes, my youth, doctor. I like to have a good
time. You probably won't believe this, but it's true.
You're the first man with whom I've talked of anything

but sickness in nearly three years. And for three years I
haven't danced, either. And how I love to dance!

ZUBIAGA: There's a dance at the club every month.

JOSEPHINE: Yes, for the upper-class people of the village.
But you mustn't forget those people call me a quack
doctor. At Carnival time, the mayor offered to take me
to the Municipal dance, but of course in costume and
wearing a mask. I waited for him till two o'clock in the
morning. And he never came. Afterward he told me he
had been ill. Just an excuse! I had to put back into my
trunk my Colombine costume with all its lace that I had
worked so hard to make. It's still there, waiting for the
moths and laughing itself to pieces. (*pause*) And look
at this dress. Eight months ago I ordered it from Buenos
Aires, so happy and thrilled. Today is the first day I've
put it on. When I think about it, I feel like crying.
(*with an abrupt change*) Another glass, doctor? Come
on. Join me. It makes a person forget. It chases away the
blues.

ZUBIAGA: If you insist . . .

JOSEPHINE: Let's drink to the success of your next play.
May this one have a run of three hundred nights!

ZUBIAGA: What? How did you know that I . . .

JOSEPHINE: I read the newspapers, doctor. I know that last
year your play was a big success in Buenos Aires. *God
Comes in Through the Window.* Accept my congratulations, though they come a bit late.

ZUBIAGA: Thank you.

JOSEPHINE: Are you working on another play for this year?

ZUBIAGA: Well, I have an idea, but I'm still looking for the
main character. One of these days . . .

JOSEPHINE: Then I drink to your discovery of a character.
Here's to it!

ZUBIAGA: Thank you. (*getting up*) It's been a pleasure.
But I mustn't delay you longer. At what time will you
finish here?

JOSEPHINE: At seven, doctor.

ZUBIAGA: Then if it's convenient with you, I'll meet you at the Rosales house at seven-thirty.

JOSEPHINE (*disillusioned*):   At his house? You're just like the mayor.

ZUBIAGA: In what way?

JOSEPHINE: You're quick to regret. A few minutes ago you were going to come for me in your car.

ZUBIAGA: If you want . . .

JOSEPHINE: No, I understand. I don't want to cause you embarrassment. At seven-thirty at the home of Indalecio Rosales, then.

ZUBIAGA: Very well. I'll never forget this pleasant moment that you have given me.

JOSEPHINE: Neither shall I, doctor. (*She remains motionless, looking at him.*)

ZUBIAGA: May I have my hat?

JOSEPHINE: Oh, yes. Excuse me. (*She hands him his hat. She helps him into his overcoat after pulling out the tip of his handkerchief from a pocket. All is done slowly, as if with an unconscious wish to prolong the visit.*)

ZUBIAGA: Thank you. Goodbye, Sister Josephine.

JOSEPHINE: Goodbye, brother doctor. (*She accompanies him to the door.*) This way. (*She opens it and watches after he has disappeared. She smiles and waves a farewell. Then she closes the door. After a moment, enter Manuel, left.*)

MANUEL: Miss Josephine. There are a lot of patients waiting. You'd better start seeing them.

JOSEPHINE: Oh, Manuel, how I like that man! How I like him!

(*Manuel stares at her, shaking his head.*)

CURTAIN

Scene 2

The same scene six weeks later. As the curtain rises,
Josephine is seated in a comfortable arm chair. In the back-
ground can be heard a radio playing an American waltz. She
is consulting a heavy book on a portable stand. On the arm
of the chair are a notebook and pencil. There is a silence,
suddenly broken by the sound of an automobile horn, com-
ing nearer. Finally the noise is deafening. Josephine gets up
in alarm.

JOSEPHINE: What's that? What's the matter?

MANUEL *(rushing in)* :   Oh, Josephine! Eureka! Eureka!

JOSEPHINE: Have you gone crazy?

MANUEL: I'll bet you don't know what happened!

JOSEPHINE: It must be something terribly important.

MANUEL *(throwing open the window)* :   Look! Look! *(Ges-*
turing outside) I went out to collect a bill of five
hundred pesos and I come back with a seven thousand
peso automobile. Look, with radio and everything.

JOSEPHINE *(at the window)* :   Marvelous!

MANUEL: Given up by the doctors. With one foot in the
coffin. And I just saw him in front of the church talking
with the priest. You saved his life. All over town they're
talking of nothing else.
(The Waltz has ended on the radio. Now the voice of
the Announcer is heard.)

ANNOUNCER: This is Radio L.O.K. Flash! On account of
numerous complaints, the Provincial Department of
Health is announcing a step-up in its campaign against
unlicensed medical practitioners and quack doctors. Orders have been sent to all police departments . . .

MANUEL: Turn that off, Pancho! Push the switch. *(The*
radio is silenced. Josephine hangs her head. Manuel
closes the window.) What? Don't you let that worry you.
At the moment when you've just received the highest

payment in your whole career. Let the government protest. And the Health Department and the doctors, too! We're providing happiness and health here. But tell me, Josephine. Tell me the truth. What did you do for Indalecio Rosales?

JOSEPHINE: Nothing. He cured himself. If I hadn't gone there, he'd still have recovered. It was just coincidence. My good luck. But I wish I'd never seen him, Manuel.

MANUEL: On account of Zubiaga?

JOSEPHINE: Yes, poor Zubiaga!

MANUEL: He's in trouble, that fellow. He's washed up. Nobody will call on him now, not even to cure a cold. They say he's leaving town.

JOSEPHINE: No! He can't!

MANUEL: That's right. As the last straw, they've even fired him as coroner and police doctor.

JOSEPHINE: What for?

MANUEL: On account of what he said about the death of Gutiérrez. Zubiaga insisted that Ponizio shot him from the front.

JOSEPHINE: That's the way it was.

MANUEL: Maybe so, but the mayor says it was from the rear.

JOSEPHINE: That's slander.

MANUEL: Well, what do you care? If Zubiaga leaves, you have one enemy less in the village.

JOSEPHINE: No, I swear he's not going to leave. Not for anything in the world! The mayor must reappoint him. Some way or other, with one excuse or other. Otherwise . . .

MANUEL: Otherwise, what?

JOSEPHINE: There'll be war, Manuel! War. (*The phone rings.*)

MANUEL: But, Josephine . . .

JOSEPHINE: Answer the phone.

MANUEL: But you mustn't . . .

JOSEPHINE: Answer the phone!

MANUEL (*aside as he picks up the phone*):   Confound it! I'm afraid you're getting too fond of him! Hello. What is it, Pancho? What? (*to Josephine*) It's that man.

JOSEPHINE: Who?

MANUEL: Zubiaga. He wants to know if you'll see him.

JOSEPHINE (*completely changed and excited*):   Yes. Right away. Tell him to come right in. And leave us alone, Manuel. Don't come back till I call you.

MANUEL: Hm! I don't like this at all. (*Exit left, shaking his head. Josephine fixes her hair rapidly in front of a mirror. She puts rouge on her lips. Reenter Manuel, left, followed by Zubiaga.*) Come in, doctor. (*Enter Zubiaga. Manuel looks at Josephine before going out, right.*)

JOSEPHINE: Come in, doctor. (*extending her hand*) How are you?

ZUBIAGA (*in a low voice*):   All right. (*She reaches for his hat.*) Thanks, but don't bother. I'll be only a minute.

JOSEPHINE (*insisting*):   Oh, permit me. (*She takes his hat and puts it on the rack.*) Sit down, doctor. (*Zubiaga takes a seat. He is changed from his previous visit. It is easy to see he is worried. He is pale. His expression is one of deep sorrow.*) What may I do for you?

ZUBIAGA: I'm going to be frank, señorita. For two weeks, my life has been impossible. I'm completely upset. I've come to settle my doubts. I had to know what you found wrong with Indalecio Rosales, so I came to ask you.

JOSEPHINE: To ask? Me?

ZUBIAGA (*irritated*):   Well, you cured him, didn't you? That's evident. That much I realize. I confess there was an error in my diagnosis. Not only mine, but all my colleagues. What was wrong?

JOSEPHINE (*ironically*):   A malignant tumor.

ZUBIAGA (*angrily*):   No! No, it wasn't a malignant tumor. You know that. If it had been, you couldn't have cured him. So evidently we were all wrong.

JOSEPHINE: Except me.

ZUBIAGA: That's right. Except you. But if you were able to cure him, it was because you found out what was wrong with him. Don't try to make me believe in miracles. I have no use for them.

JOSEPHINE *(calmly)*: But when a person can't explain the reason for something, it's necessary to give it a name. In the eyes of the family of Indalecio Rosales and of everybody in the village, Sister Josephine worked a miracle and cured his cancer. Of course, I know he didn't have one.

ZUBIAGA *(raising his voice)*: Then what did he have? You must tell me what he did have.

JOSEPHINE: What do you mean, "must"?

ZUBIAGA *(subsiding)*: I beg your pardon.

JOSEPHINE: Calm yourself, doctor. You're too excited. I'm willing to do as you ask and I'll tell you anything you want to know. But don't shout like that, I beg you.

ZUBIAGA: I'm upset. My nerves . . .

JOSEPHINE: I understand. *(silence)* So then, you want to know what was the matter with him.

ZUBIAGA: If that's agreeable with you.

JOSEPHINE: Perfectly. His trouble was hunger.

ZUBIAGA: Hunger?

JOSEPHINE: That's true. Hunger. Without realizing it, all of you were killing him with his diet.

ZUBIAGA: You're mocking me!

JOSEPHINE: Not at all. At first I thought his case was hopeless, especially since you gave him a week to live. And since he was condemned to die, and since everybody respects the last wishes of a condemned man. . . .

ZUBIAGA: What was his last wish?

JOSEPHINE: An artichoke omelet, doctor.

ZUBIAGA: You're making a fool of me!

JOSEPHINE: No, doctor. That's what he asked for. And I ordered them to give it to him, so that he'd get what he

wanted and at least die contented. Then since the omelet didn't kill him, I followed it with garlic soup. And
after that, chicken, and a sweet desert. And now there
he is, alive and wiggling.

ZUBIAGA *(again excited)* : I know what you fed him. But
first you gave him powders every day. Powders dissolved
in his tea. And you used to visit the patient and send everybody out of the room. What were you doing with him?

JOSEPHINE: I don't suppose you imagine I was making love
to him. After all, he's seventy years old.

ZUBIAGA: I know what you were doing: giving him injections!

JOSEPHINE: Don't say that, doctor.

ZUBIAGA: Well, you were! *(taking a glass phial from his
pocket)* I've got one of the capsules.

JOSEPHINE: You have an excellent spy system.

ZUBIAGA: So you confess it, do you?

JOSEPHINE: Why shouldn't I confess the truth?

ZUBIAGA: Well, then, what were the injections?

JOSEPHINE: Water, doctor.

ZUBIAGA: Water?

JOSEPHINE: That's right. Water. I told him it was mor-
phine, and he had such faith in my words and my
suggestions that even though you may not believe it, his
pains disappeared and he smiled. That was when I suspected an error in diagnosis. That sort of pain doesn't
go away with water or diminish through suggestion, so I
gave him the food.

ZUBIAGA: Forgive me! So many things have piled up on me,
I don't know! I raise my voice without reason. I lose control over the most insignificant things.

JOSEPHINE: People tell me you are talking of leaving town.

ZUBIAGA: Yes, I'm going away.

JOSEPHINE: Why?

ZUBIAGA: On your account and on account of politics.

JOSEPHINE: Better change the order, doctor. Say rather, on

account of politics and me. What doctor would think of
disagreeing with a diagnosis of the mayor? You haven't
had much experience in politics, I'm afraid. The mayor
says Gutiérrez was killed from the rear, and that's the
way it's got to be. Are you sure that wasn't another mistake of yours?

ZUBIAGA: I didn't come here to have you make fun of me.
But it was a shot from directly in front that passed
through his kidney, perforated the aorta, and lodged in
the eleventh rib. The bullet can still be felt under the
skin.

JOSEPHINE: And where are you going?

ZUBIAGA: To Alberdi, I think. I'm waiting for a letter.

JOSEPHINE: You're making a mistake. Why give up here?

ZUBIAGA: What is there here for me? Your cure of that man
was spectacular. For three months people had been asking me twenty times a day: "How's Rosales?" And I kept
replying: "Bad. Very ill. There's nothing can be done.
It's terminal." And then you came along and six weeks
later he throws me out and shouts: "Sister Josephine
cured me. Zubiaga is a murderer who was starving me to
death!" Why, they laugh in my face! In the club, in the
street. I can't take it. If I don't get out of here by tomorrow, I'll have an attack of something.

JOSEPHINE: To think I did you all that harm unintention-
ally!

ZUBIAGA: You did what you thought necessary. I'm not re-
proaching you. I would be an idiot to put all the blame
on you. It's partly my own doing. I came into the world
condemned to failure. When I opened practice in Brand-
zen, my first case was an unfortunate birth. The poor
mother died. I had to go somewhere else, and on and on,
like a wandering cowboy. That's the history of my professional life. And in my private life I've been just as unfortunate. In Balcarce two years ago I fell very much in love

and got married, secretly hoping that my change in status would change everything. But she died six months
later. Poor girl! (*pause*) And bad luck still follows me.
Now, just when I was beginning to build a practice that
this month brought me a thousand pesos, this happens.
If it weren't so tragic, it would be a joke.

JOSEPHINE: Her death must have been a great sorrow.

ZUBIAGA: There wasn't anybody like her in the world.
(*opening the cover of his watch*) Here's her picture.
Only nineteen years old. (*Josephine leans toward him to
look at the photograph.*) An angel. Full of life. So pretty.
One Sunday we went into the country to spend the day.
That night when we got back, she had a fever. The next
day, temperature 104. Typhoid. She didn't live ten days.
It's not fair! I tell you I was ready to shoot myself. But
forgive me! I don't know how I happened to tell you all
this.

JOSEPHINE: I'm glad you did, doctor. There are things a
person has to tell somebody to feel better. That often
happens to me. (*Telephone rings.*) Excuse me, doctor.
I must answer. It won't take long. (*Opens her box of cig-
arets.*) Here. Smoke one. It'll calm your nerves.

ZUBIAGA (*lighting one*) :   Thank you.

JOSEPHINE: Hello. Yes, this is Sister Josephine. Yes. Hello,
Scotti. How? And when was that? Last night? Oh. Uh
huh! Nose still bleeding? Uh Huh. And still in jail? Yes,
I'll look after it. (*to Zubiaga*) Excuse me for a minute
more. (*at the phone*) Police station. (*to Zubiaga*) How
are the nerves? Better? (*Zubiaga laughs.*) Oh, hello.
How are you, Mr. Commissioner? I'm always bothering
you. Oh, so you can guess why I'm calling. Yes, he's a
good lad. A bit flighty. A patient of mine. Broke the
bone of his nose? Oh, that can be arranged, Mr. Commissioner. And remember the Galíndez family has eight
brothers and cousins. Yes, and at least seventeen friends.

Mustn't lose all those votes. Yes, if you'll release him. Let him take his siesta at home today. Thank you. Call on me if you . . . Yes, I know. Goodbye. (*Hangs up.*)

ZUBIAGA: You seem quite friendly with the Commissioner of Police.

JOSEPHINE: With everybody, Doctor Zubiaga. With the mayor, too. Would you like me to talk to him?

ZUBIAGA: Thank you. It would be a waste of time.

JOSEPHINE: Don't jump to conclusions. The Mayor always listens to me. He is considerably in debt for my help.

ZUBIAGA: If you talked to him for me, I'd be in debt to you, too, and I won't be indebted to anybody. Besides, I've made up my mind to get away from here.

JOSEPHINE: I still think you should stay.

ZUBIAGA: What interest is it of yours?

JOSEPHINE: I regret your leaving. I suspect that you and I could become friends, and friends are scarce around here.

ZUBIAGA: Yet I hear that quite respectable people come to see you.

JOSEPHINE: Like whom?

ZUBIAGA: The mayor.

JOSEPHINE: Yes, we chat. Night before last he was here till quite late. He wasn't very happy when he left. In the voting list there are six hundred names that I control, and obviously that bothers him. He knows they might cause trouble.

ZUBIAGA: And how do you manage to control six hundred votes?

JOSEPHINE: People who are grateful to me, doctor. Some I've cured, some I've treated free. Others have used letters of recommendation from me when they went to Buenos Aires. I've given money to a few, and the rest are afraid of me. You see, doctor, I'm not like you. I compromise. I provide the mayor with votes and then, though there may be a local complaint or two, he doesn't bother me.

ZUBIAGA: It's a matter of the thickness of one's skin. Even if I wanted to, I couldn't bring myself around to it. I have my principles.

JOSEPHINE: You wouldn't find it hard. Do you know what I'd do if I were you? I'd go and talk to the mayor. Why don't you let me arrange an appointment? (*Points to the telephone.*)

ZUBIAGA (*getting up*) : Don't bother. I'm leaving. I want no part in it.

JOSEPHINE: You're stubborn, doctor. Think it over. When you start earning a thousand pesos a month, things are looking up. You've got a start. People will soon forget the Rosales incident, just as they have forgotten the September revolution. Stay here, doctor.

ZUBIAGA: There's only one reason I'd stay: to get him and his cronies out of office.

JOSEPHINE: I like that, doctor. I like the sort of man who gets angry and demands action. It's easy enough to overthrow the mayor. If I joined with you . . . (*struck by a sudden idea*) Tell me, doctor, do you want me to get you elected mayor?

ZUBIAGA: You're out of your mind.

JOSEPHINE: I could easily fix it.

ZUBIAGA: I don't doubt that.

JOSEPHINE: Well, then, answer my question.

ZUBIAGA: No, I don't want to be mayor.

JOSEPHINE: Why not?

ZUBIAGA: Because my first act would have to be to drive you out of town. And I'm not capable of such treachery. So let's not discuss it. My hat, please. (*Josephine takes it from the rack, but still holds it.*)

JOSEPHINE: I could have him reappoint you coroner against your wishes.

ZUBIAGA: I'd resign.

JOSEPHINE: I'd like to see you.

ZUBIAGA: You're very boastful about your power. You could very well fail.

JOSEPHINE: I'd like to see that.

ZUBIAGA: Well, don't ask him because I could make a lot of trouble for you.

JOSEPHINE: I'd like to see you try. And I'd like you to see what I can do when I want something. Remember, Doctor Zubiaga, you're not going to leave town.

ZUBIAGA: Who said so? Your fish?

JOSEPHINE: Yes, my precious fish that never deceive me.

ZUBIAGA: Well, just so you see that sometimes they aren't trustworthy, within forty-eight hours I'll be back here to say goodbye. Now will you kindly give me my hat?

JOSEPHINE: Oh, yes! (*She gives it to him. It is all crumpled.*) Then may I hope you'll keep your promise and come to say goodbye?

ZUBIAGA: I gave you my word. (*Shakes hands with her.*) Good afternoon, Sister Josephine.

JOSEPHINE (*shaking hands*):   Then I'll see you, brother doctor. (*She opens the door. He leaves, as in the first scene. She follows him with her eyes, then waves. She shuts the door, thinks, turns, and while she wrings her hands nervously*) No, he won't leave! He mustn't go away!

CURTAIN

ACT 2

The room in which Sister Josephine holds her séances. In the center, a three-legged table, a set of mahogany chairs. A bookcase in one corner. In another, a large, low sofa with many pillows. A switchboard for lights. A mysterious air about the room. As the curtain rises, Manuel is talking over the telephone.

MANUEL: Hello. Yes, this is Manuel. What's the matter? What's that, Anselmo? You're doing just the opposite of what the spirit told you and you're nervous? Naturally! I could understand if you had talked with some stranger, but it was the spirit of your father. He's quite likely to refuse to come the next time we summon him. Why should he come back to face suffering? You sold it? Did you sign the papers? Well, then, refuse! Don't sign anything. Make out you're a stupid foreigner. Laugh at him. The wind has already carried away your words. Tell him you had a second thought. Why not tell him the truth? The spirit of your dead father appeared and told you not to sell good land for 150 pesos an acre, with a road planned that will take you to Necochea in a couple of hours. That would be silly. How do I know? Because the dead man told me. (*Hangs up.*) You'd know, too, if you read the *Nación,* stupid! (*Opens the door.*) Be good enough to come in, doctor.

ZUBIAGA (*entering and holding his hat*) :   Good afternoon.

MANUEL: How have you been?

ZUBIAGA: Sister Josephine?

MANUEL: She'll be with you in a moment. (*Takes his hat.*) Have a seat.

ZUBIAGA (*sitting*) :   Well, I'm amazed. This house is like a fortress. So many rooms.

MANUEL: It used to be a convent.

ZUBIAGA: I never saw this room.

MANUEL: Here, doctor, is where we talk with the spirits.

ZUBIAGA: Oh, indeed. So here's where the dead people return. (*He looks about.*) How strange!

MANUEL: Yes, doctor. Some people who have to consult dead friends come here, summon them, talk with them, and take their advice.

ZUBIAGA: Does the spirit always turn up?

MANUEL: No, not always. Sometimes our best efforts fail, and the client who comes to find out whether his missing brother is dead, or with whom his runaway wife is living, goes away just as he came.

ZUBIAGA: Not just the way he came because I suppose you make him pay for your assistance.

MANUEL: Of course. Even though you may say that in fun, these sessions are a tremendous drain on Sister Josephine's spiritual force. That can't be completely repaid with money.

ZUBIAGA: I didn't know she was a medium.

MANUEL: Neither did we till one night she fell and opened her head.

ZUBIAGA: She did?

MANUEL: Yes, it happened in Coronel Suárez two years ago. We were sitting around a table with hands joined. With the help of some medium we were seeking someone who had disappeared, but the medium couldn't seem to make contact. Then all of a sudden, crash! There was Sister Josephine senseless on the floor. It was frightening. Her head hit a clothespress and opened a gash right here. (*Indicates on his own.*) It needed three stitches. But it was a revelation, and ever since . . .

ZUBIAGA: Is she pretty good as a medium?

MANUEL: She has her days. Yesterday, for instance, things didn't go very well. We were having an important séance. It lasted three hours. The poor girl was exhausted.

ZUBIAGA: You mean she worked all that time?

MANUEL: Well, you see we were trying to summon the spirit of a man that we knew had died in Italy. He left a considerable fortune that his brothers and nephews are trying to take away from his two children who so far are considered illegitimate because no one can find their birth certificates that everybody knows exist.

ZUBIAGA: So the spirit had to travel all the way from Italy?

MANUEL: No, doctor. Spirits dwell near their relatives. After they turn into spirits, they leave the spots where nobody cared about them. They seek the warmth of those who loved them in life. That's why it's so hard to summon them back.

ZUBIAGA: Do you really believe all that?

MANUEL: Why not, doctor? You laugh because you don't believe it. That's natural. There are many like you, people who have never seen a spirit. But there are many who have never seen Europe, yet they believe it exists.

ZUBIAGA: You know that's a ridiculous argument.

MANUEL: There are many who make fun of it at first. But you should see them after their first experience. People you'd never suspect sit around this table.

ZUBIAGA: Really?

MANUEL: Two months ago we could have destroyed a French legend.

ZUBIAGA: What do you mean?

MANUEL: The Unknown Soldier was here in this room, telling us how he died.

ZUBIAGA: The Unknown Soldier? The one buried in Paris under the Arch of Triumph?

MANUEL: He's the one. His name is Jean Durand.

ZUBIAGA: Jean Durand is like calling him Pedro García or John Smith.

MANUEL: As far as that goes, you're right. But suppose Jean Durand tells you he was born in Bayonne, the son of Jean Jacques Perigord and Catherine Castagnet, that he lived at 23 Rue de la Gare, and that he was part of the 78th regiment of the 136th regiment in the Chemin des Dames sector before he was shot by Hermann Wisely. Then what would you say?

ZUBIAGA (*perplexed*) :   I wish I could have heard him.

MANUEL: That's easy, doctor. He'll come whenever she summons him, because the uncle who adopted him is overseer on the Uselay Farm.

ZUBIAGA: And you say you're going to have a séance today?

MANUEL: That's right.

ZUBIAGA: To talk to that uncle from Italy?

MANUEL: That's what we hope. But it may not be so easy. In recent sessions we've had so much interference. There's one spirit that tries to make itself heard, since it has something important to tell us.

ZUBIAGA: Don't they know who it is?

MANUEL: No. We thought the spirit had something to do with the matter of the inheritance, but no. There's no connection. It seems to be the spirit of a young woman recently deceased.

ZUBIAGA: What does she say?

MANUEL: Mostly it's weeping. Apparently she's trying to prevent something she knows is going to happen, but we can't get anything definite. All she does is talk about her husband whom she must have loved a lot to be so worried about his future.

ZUBIAGA: Oh, indeed?

MANUEL: Unfortunately Sister Josephine has too little information to identify the spirit. If we only knew the name of the husband so we could tell him she wanted to talk with him.

ZUBIAGA: Do you mean put an advertisement in the newspaper: "NOTICE. To a recent widower. Somebody wants to talk to you from the next world." Are you sure you don't know any names?

MANUEL: None.

ZUBIAGA: Then the next time she turns up, ask her. (*Enter Josephine, looking very lovely in a white dress.*)

JOSEPHINE (*extending her hand*): Hello, doctor. How are you?

ZUBIAGA: (*getting up to shake her hand*): Fine, thank you, and you?

JOSEPHINE: Just as you see me. Always busy. Manuel, tell the people out there to wait just a minute. We'll start very soon.

MANUEL: I'll tell them, Sister. (*Exit Manuel.*)

ZUBIAGA: Forgive me if I come at an inconvenient time.

JOSEPHINE: Not at all, doctor.

ZUBIAGA: Manuel tells me you're about to have a . . . **well**
. . . that is . . . a session of . . .

JOSEPHINE: Yes, of spiritualism. A séance.

ZUBIAGA: Yes, and that your clients are waiting. But since I
gave you my word of honor to come and say
goodbye . . .

JOSEPHINE: So you're still determined to go away?

ZUBIAGA: Absolutely.

JOSEPHINE: Where?

ZUBIAGA: Alberdi.

JOSEPHINE: When?

ZUBIAGA: Tonight.

JOSEPHINE (*after a short silence*):   Well, what can we do
about it if that's the way you want it? May you have a
pleasant trip and lots of luck. I wish you all the success
that anyone can want. And don't forget that you're
leaving a friend always ready to serve you.

ZUBIAGA: Thank you. You express my feelings, too.

JOSEPHINE: When does your train leave?

ZUBIAGA: Ten o'clock.

JOSEPHINE: Then there's plenty of time. You've got two
hours.

ZUBIAGA: Well, I still have a few things to do.

JOSEPHINE: Like sending your trunk to the station?

ZUBIAGA: Exactly.

JOSEPHINE: That won't take more than ten minutes. We
can talk for a bit. I want to toast your departure in
champagne. I hope you won't turn me down.

ZUBIAGA: What a way to put it!

JOSEPHINE: Will you wait in my study till I finish with my
clients? It shouldn't take fifteen minutes, if all goes well.
I'm not very hopeful, though. I'm a bit upset today. But
anyway, I'll do my best. You can wait right next door
unless you want to sit in on the experiment.

ZUBIAGA: No, thank you. I'd prefer the study.

JOSEPHINE: As you wish. That's what I'd prefer, too. I mean about you. When I'm in a trance, I've got to be completely tranquil, and your presence would be a disturbing factor.

ZUBIAGA: Really? Do you think so?

JOSEPHINE: Yes, indeed. I might fail again as I did the other night. And that would be a shame. These people have come from so far away. And they're so full of hope. To defraud them would be a crime!

ZUBIAGA: Well, perhaps I'd like to see that. It would be very interesting. However . . .

JOSEPHINE: You're saying you'd like to, but you don't dare. You're afraid.

ZUBIAGA: Afraid? Not at all.

JOSEPHINE: Perhaps I exaggerated when I said "afraid." It's childish to be afraid of the dead. But there are people who don't like to think about spirits. I suppose you are one of them.

ZUBIAGA: Not me. It's just that I don't believe in all this.

JOSEPHINE: You don't have to believe, doctor. You can be merely a silent witness. Why should I try to turn you into a believer? If it's because you're afraid you'll be recognized, don't worry. As I said, these people have come from far away. But do as you wish. It doesn't matter. I'll have them come in. If you're uneasy about staying, there's my study. If you want to stay, sit over there and be good enough to look and listen with respect as even the irreligious look and listen at a mass. (*turning to the door*) Manuel, show them in. (*Zubiaga, as if obedient to some external force, goes to the chair she has indicated and sits down. Josephine, rigid, throws back her head an instant. Enter Manuel, followed by a woman and a man.*)

MANUEL: Come in. Take seats, please.

MAN (*in a definitely Italian dialect*) : Well, let's see, Sister

Josephine, if you can get somewhere today. The lawyer
pushes, pushes. He needs the facts to make his claim,
and we're losing time.

MANUEL: Please, sir, don't talk to the medium. (*Meanwhile Manuel is extinguishing the lights, leaving only
one that shines on Josephine. Zubiaga's chair is in the
deep shadow. There is more illumination on the clients
as they take seats. Manuel stands near Josephine, who
appears to be in a trance.*)

WOMAN (*also in Italian dialect*): For two weeks we spent
nearly every day here and you know how far we've
come.

MAN: And yet we haven't talked to the dead man.

WOMAN: She sits at the table, a thump here, a thump there.

MAN: The table moved. It said yes; it said no.

WOMAN: But it never said where the birth certificate was.

MAN: And time is getting short.

MANUEL: You must have patience. It's not a matter of
summoning a dead man and having him come right
away. It's hard work. Since we've not been able to learn
anything with the table, we've got to materialize him.

WOMAN: Suppose he doesn't want to materialize?

MAN: I don't understand.

MANUEL: Please keep silent. With all this talk you'll only
upset the medium. Come. Stand beside me. It's time to
make the chain. Take hands. Yes, that's the way. Near
the Sister. Now everybody concentrate. (*pause*) Calmly.
(*silence*) Don't you feel anything?

WOMAN: What?

MANUEL: Like a gentle breeze?

WOMAN: No. I don't.

MAN: I do. Someone is squeezing my hand.

MANUEL: Silence! Sister Josephine is concentrating. Something is taking possession of her. That's why her hand
trembles. Even from here I can hear how her heart is

pounding. Bring her a chair. Quick! (*The man brings a chair. Sister Josephine sinks into it as if asleep.*) What is the name of the dead man?

MAN: Francesco.

WOMAN: We already told you that twenty times.

MANUEL: That's true. Francesco Caporale. (*silence*) Francesco! Are you Francesco Caporale? Answer. You are among friends. Here are your two children, who can't inherit your property because they can't find their birth certificates. In what church were they baptized? Please tell them. Answer. (*silence*)

MAN: He don't say nothing.

WOMAN: Just like the other days.

MANUEL: Perhaps because he doesn't recognize my voice. Why don't one of you speak to him? Speak affectionately.

MAN: Chicho! Are you there, Chicho? This is Juanín talking. I'm fine here. How are you? We're always thinking about you. We love you a lot. Are you there, Chicho? (*Josephine moans.*)

MANUEL: Wait! The Sister is suffering. It looks as though she wanted to talk and someone won't let her. Who are you? I order you to reply.

JOSEPHINE: Let me alone! Let me alone!

WOMAN: What's the matter?

MAN: Nobody is touching her.

MANUEL: Silence! Two spirits are trying to materialize. That often happens. They fight in her body. The strongest one will win out.

JOSEPHINE: Let me alone! (*with a sigh of relief*) Oh!

MANUEL: There! One of them has materialized. Now we'll find out who it is. Is that you, Chicho?

JOSEPHINE (*in a deep masculine voice*):   Sono io, Giuseppe Caporale. Morto a Praga nel 1930. Chi mi chiama? (It's I. Guiseppe Caporale. I died in Prague in 1930. Who is calling me?)

WOMAN: Carmela.

MAN: And Juanín.

JOSEPHINE: Carmela e Juanín? Figli miei! che volete da
me? (Carmela and Juanín? My children! What do you
want of me?)

WOMAN: Our proof of birth. Where is it? Do you know?

JOSEPHINE: Lo so. (I know.)

MAN: Where is it, then?

JOSEPHINE: Nella chiesa di San Antonio di Padova. Ma
non la cercate. Inutile! Non esiste! Il bombardamento
austriaco l'ha incendiata. Tutto e scomparso. L'atto di
nascita non si troverá mai più! Mai più! (In the church
at St. Anthony of Padua. But don't go looking for it!
Useless! It doesn't exist. The Austrian bombardment
burned it up. It's all gone. The birth certificate will
never be found. Never!)

MAN: Virgin help us!

WOMAN: Is that true? (*Sister Josephine faints.*)

MANUEL: Sister! Sister! She's fainted. Help me put her on
the sofa.

(*Josephine is motionless. Zubiaga still sits in his chair.*)

MANUEL: Sister! (*He shakes her.*) Don't worry. It's all
over. The spirit has dematerialized.

WOMAN: What's the matter?

MANUEL (*slapping Josephine's cheek*): He won't come
back.

MAN: Is she dead?

MANUEL: Don't talk nonsense! We'll just have to leave her
here for a moment until she recovers. Her effort was too
great.

WOMAN: There's nothing we can do, eh?

MAN: If the church burned, there go our hopes for the
inheritance.

MANUEL: What can I say? Everything possible has been
done. You have spoken with your dead father.

WOMAN: He didn't tell us much.

MANUEL: He told you what you wanted to know. I'm only sorry it was bad news.

MAN: And now what about paying?

WOMAN: How much?

MANUEL: Come back tomorrow. You can talk about it with the Sister. This isn't the proper moment.

MAN: Then until tomorrow!

WOMAN (*as she starts out*): That's fantastic. Fantastic! That was Chicho. He talked in Italian and everything.

MAN: What did you expect him to do? But I don't believe it. (*Exeunt both.*)

MANUEL: Josephine! Doctor, please help me! (*Patting her hand.*) Sister!

ZUBIAGA (*who has turned on the light, approaches her skeptically*): Strange! (*He examines her with a smile of disbelief.*) Didn't you say this had happened before? That you just have to wait till she recovers?

MANUEL (*in trembling voice*): Never like this. Never so long. She usually recovers right away. But she's so pale and cold.

ZUBIAGA: Give me a match.

MANUEL: What are you going to do, doctor? (*Zubiaga does not reply, and continues staring at her. Manuel finally hands him a box of matches. He lights one and brings it near her eyes. She does not move.*)

ZUBIAGA: That's strange. She doesn't blink. Do you have a pin?

MANUEL: Doctor, I'm frightened. Nothing like this has ever happened. (*The doctor takes her pulse. He slaps her cheek. Manuel hands him a pin.*) Here, doctor.

ZUBIAGA: Give me it. (*He sticks it into the palm of her hand. Josephine does not move. Zubiaga, who had thought at first that this was a put-up job, seems uncertain.*) Hurry to my house, Manuel. Tell them to give you my case of injections and two vials of camphorated oil. Hurry!

MANUEL: Is it very serious, doctor?

ZUBIAGA: Hurry! Run! (*Manuel runs out. Zubiaga remains beside Josephine, who appears to be dead. He raises her, then sits her up. Her head falls back. Then Zubiaga lays her back on the sofa. He lights another match. He takes her hand and brings the flame near her palm. Josephine utters a cry of pain. Then while he keeps observing her, she sits up slowly and passes her other hand across her forehead. She sighs.*)

ZUBIAGA: How are you? Feeling better?

JOSEPHINE (*in a far-away voice and without opening her eyes*) :   Darling! Where are you? I'm sure you are near? I can feel you. I know you're near, but I can't reach you. For a year I've traveled through the shadows to reach you. And I suffer and agonize, but I can't make you hear me. A year that seems like a thousand! But I must reach you! My soul lives only through the memory of you. It can't be in vain that I follow you, inspire you, protect you.

ZUBIAGA: All right! That's enough! I won't be a party to this farce a minute longer. Wake up! Talk! Explain yourself. What's your idea in doing this to me? Why do you mock me like this? (*Josephine opens her eyes.*)

JOSEPHINE: Calm yourself, Armando. You always get so upset. This is I . . . Your Leticia. The wife you adore.

ZUBIAGA: That's a lie!

JOSEPHINE: Don't insult her. She doesn't hear you. Josephine no longer exists. She's only an instrument. I have taken over her body, Taken over her eyes to see you, her tongue to speak to you. I'm Leticia, your wife. Leti, you used to call me, remember? My chestnut hair, my green eyes, my gold tooth. My happy laugh always trying to cure your bitter sadness. The first present you ever gave

me was a book of poetry. Baudelaire. I can still see its
black leather cover with the gold letters, and that poem
you circled with a red pencil: "Spleen." "I am a ceme-
tery hated by the moon," it began. We burned the book
together in the fireplace one winter night because I was
trying to cure your melancholy. Surely you remember.

ZUBIAGA: Leti! Leti! No, I don't believe. I can't believe!

JOSEPHINE: Remember the first time we ever saw each
other? In October. In the plaza at Santa Rosalía Fair. I
was all in white, and in charge of a booth raffling off
dolls. You bought all the chances and didn't get a single
doll. How we laughed about that!

ZUBIAGA: No. Hush! It's horrible. What you're saying is
horrible!

JOSEPHINE: The night of our marriage, when we entered
the bedroom, you couldn't find the light switch. I
groped around and fell over a table and knocked it
down. When you finally turned on the light, there we
stood looking at each other in terror. I had just broken
a mirror . . .

ZUBIAGA: Leti! Leti, is it really you? Really?

JOSEPHINE: A week before I got ill, we were both in the
winter garden. It was a clear, moonlit night. The open
window looked onto the park. I was playing the piano
and you had your eyes closed. Mendelssohn, remember?
"The Spring Song." (She hums a few bars.) Your eyes
were full of tears, the way they are now. You took me in
your arms and kissed me . . .

ZUBIAGA: Leti, yes, I believe you. Forgive me. Forgive me
for doubting. But hearing you speak, reminding me of
intimate things that no one else could know, it's enough
to drive me crazy. (He falls to his knees beside the sofa
where Josephine is lying and weeps.)

JOSEPHINE (caressing his head with her hands):   Calm
yourself, darling. You're upset. Realize that my soul has
found you at last. From now on, I'll surround you like a

shadow. I'll protect and inspire you. When life envelops you with its pain and despair, call me. I'll be with you forever, as I am now. Adiós, Armando.

ZUBIAGA: Leti! Darling Leti! Don't go away! There's so much I want to ask you. You can't leave me like this, with my soul so upset. Leti! Leti! (*He is sobbing. Enter Manuel with a box of injections. He stops. Noticing his presence, Zubiaga gets up. His mortal blow has left him shaken. He is stunned.*)

MANUEL: Doctor, what's the matter? You're crying.

ZUBIAGA: Don't ask me anything. What has happened is so ridiculous. Yes, I'm crying. Why deny it? Everything was so sudden and unexpected. I've had such a shock. It was she. I've been talking to her.

MANUEL: To whom, doctor?

ZUBIAGA: To my wife. She reminded me of things in our life that no one else could possibly know. Maybe it was only autosuggestion, but I recognized her voice, her calm expression, her tranquil smile. Now I can no longer laugh at you.

MANUEL: Hush! She's reviving. She knows nothing of all this. If you want to talk to your wife again, the medium must not know about anything. If the emotion gets transferred to Sister Josephine, your wife will never be able to materialize again. Speak to her as if nothing had happened.

JOSEPHINE (*sleepily*): Manuel, who's there?

MANUEL: Doctor Zubiaga.

JOSEPHINE: What happened to my hand that it hurts so much? It feels as if I got burned. Why, I've got a blister! (*A silence. Zubiaga and Manuel look at each other.*) What happened?

MANUEL: While you were in a trance, the Italian came up to you and dropped his cigar.

JOSEPHINE: Did they find out what they wanted to know?

MANUEL: Yes, Sister.

JOSEPHINE: Have they gone?

MANUEL: They just left.

JOSEPHINE: And what did you think of the séance, doctor?

ZUBIAGA: Very strange.

JOSEPHINE: If there was some scientific aspect about it that interested you, I'd be glad to try to answer any of your questions.

ZUBIAGA: Just one thing. Can you tell me whom you materialized?

JOSEPHINE: No. When I go into a trance, my head feels like lead. Right away my memory leaves me. When I recover, there's a sensation of having been dead for awhile, for all I can remember about anything. You see! I got a bad burn and I've felt the pain for only a couple of minutes.

ZUBIAGA (*looking at her hand*) :   Does it hurt very much?

JOSEPHINE: Terribly! But I know the remedy. Will power. Oh, that reminds me. Manuel, bring some champagne.

ZUBIAGA (*picking up his hat*) :   No, thank you. We'll drink a toast some other day. Tomorrow, or the next day. Not now. I couldn't.

JOSEPHINE: Tomorrow or the next day? What do you mean? Aren't you leaving tonight?

ZUBIAGA (*definitely*) :   No!

JOSEPHINE: Doctor, how happy you make me! My little fish, my precious fish that never deceive me! But five minutes ago you were so determined. What has happened in five minutes to make you change your mind?

ZUBIAGA (*visibly shaken*) :   Ask your fish. If it's true they never deceive you, they'll tell you why Doctor Zubiaga is going to stay in this village forever. But don't ask me. I'm so confused that I don't know. My veins seem about to burst. And I'm sure I'm going out of my mind. (*Josephine looks at Manuel in astonishment. Zubiaga gets control of himself. In calmer tones*) Excuse this outburst. But I don't know. I haven't been feeling well. Tomorrow I'll be calmer and perhaps, then . . .

JOSEPHINE: I don't understand.

ZUBIAGA (*extending his hand*) :   Sister.

JOSEPHINE (*shaking hands*) :   Until tomorrow, then.

ZUBIAGA: Until tomorrow. Goodbye, Manuel.

MANUEL (*bowing*) :   Doctor. (*Exit Zubiaga. After closing the door behind him, Manuel turns to Josephine.*) Marvelous! Stupendous! I still don't believe it.

JOSEPHINE: How much did you see?

MANUEL: Nothing, but I heard it all over the loud speaker. I sent Pancho after his box. I swear your performance moved me. I still have gooseflesh. He's set. Set. He won't go away. From now on, his life will be directed from here. He won't have a moment of peace, waiting for the next time he can talk with that spirit.

JOSEPHINE: No, Manuel, no! It's infamous! It's criminal. It can't be. I've gone too far. I was crazy. If he ever finds out what a farce it was, instead of winning his love, I'll be a target for his eternal hatred.

MANUEL: Who says it was a farce? Who says it wasn't the spirit of his wife that really inspired everything? Perhaps there was a strange force behind you, guiding you. The love you feel for him has given such tenderness to your words, such serenity to your eyes, such warmth to your hands! I, who heard you, believe that it was his wife who spoke through you.

JOSEPHINE: No, Manuel! I'm frightened. It's horrible. It's too much. Tomorrow I'm leaving for Buenos Aires.

MANUEL: But don't you love him?

JOSEPHINE: Of course I love him. Madly. For the rest of my life! Forever! But don't you see? I want him to be mine. Mine! Not like this. Now he'll come to me because of the dead woman. I'll have a dead woman as my rival. And everybody will suffer. But he most of all. He'll

suffer deeply. And I don't want that. I don't want him
to suffer. (*She falls sobbing onto the sofa.*)

CURTAIN

ACT 3

*Another room in Josephine's house. (Or the room of
Act I, if the chest is added.) A big desk. A book case. A chest
set in a conspicuous place. A door down stage. Windows at
the corner. Doors on both sides. As the curtain rises, Manuel
is pacing the floor with long steps, his hands behind him.
Josephine enters, left.*

JOSEPHINE (*anxiously*) :   Did he call?

MANUEL: Yes, twice.

JOSEPHINE: Did you tell him I was still ill?

MANUEL: Yes.

JOSEPHINE: Did he say anything?

MANUEL: That I wasn't telling him the truth. That you
were just refusing to see him.

JOSEPHINE: What did you tell him?

MANUEL: To come and see for himself if he wanted. That
for three days you had been in bed with a temperature.

JOSEPHINE: He's quite capable of coming.

MANUEL: All the better.

JOSEPHINE: No, no! I don't want to see him. I'm leaving.
This very night. My trunk is ready to go to the station.

MANUEL: Where are you going?

JOSEPHINE: To Buenos Aires.

MANUEL: For how long?

JOSEPHINE: Forever.

MANUEL: Don't you know what he'll say?

JOSEPHINE: I don't want to work any more. I'm giving it
up.

MANUEL: It doesn't seem possible that just on account of
one man . . .

JOSEPHINE: Yes, on account of one man. If Zubiaga insists once more on seeing me, I'm afraid I can't refuse. And that would be impossible. Impossible!

MANUEL: Why, impossible?

JOSEPHINE: Don't you realize that he is coming because he wants to speak with his dead wife? I'd have to go through that miserable farce again, and I couldn't.

MANUEL: Why not? You did it beautifully. Are you making up your mind to lose him because you won't make a small compromise?

JOSEPHINE: He doesn't think of me. All he thinks of is his Leticia. But that's not the trouble. The whole affair was infamous. I'll never stop being sorry I started it. And if I see him, it will be only to confess to him the whole truth. And *that* I can't do. He may never love me, but I can't stand his hating me. So it's better for me to go away. (*The telephone rings. A silence. The phone rings again. They look at each other. Josephine makes a gesture.*) Answer it. (*Manuel picks up the receiver.*)

MANUEL: Hello. What? Yes, doctor. Sister Josephine? Just a moment, please.

JOSEPHINE: Tell him I'm still in bed with a fever. (*As Manuel starts to deliver her message, she stops him.*) Wait! Give it to me. (*She takes the phone.*) Hello. How are you doctor? Oh, better, I guess. No fever, but I'm still weak. What? See you now? Hm . . . Well . . . Where are you? In the outer office? Yes, very well. (*Hangs up.*)

MANUEL: What are you going to tell him?

JOSEPHINE: The truth.

MANUEL: Oh, no! You mustn't do that. If you do, you're out of your mind.

JOSEPHINE: Leave me alone.

MANUEL: But have you considered what . . . ?

JOSEPHINE: I know what I'm doing.

MANUEL: Very well. (*Exit Manuel.*)

JOSEPHINE (*at the rear door*) :   Come in, doctor.

ZUBIAGA (*entering*) :   Good morning.

JOSEPHINE: How are you?

ZUBIAGA: That's what I should ask you. They told me you'd been ill all week. Your face doesn't show it.

JOSEPHINE: Thanks to make-up. All false and put on. Just beauty treatment.

ZUBIAGA: So you're feeling better?

JOSEPHINE: Oh, yes. Sit down. (*Zubiaga takes a seat. Silence. In a trembling voice*) What brings you here, doctor?

ZUBIAGA: Did you get my letter?

JOSEPHINE: Yes, and I was really amazed. I never knew that I was the intermediary for . . . for . . .

ZUBIAGA (*nervously interrupting her*) :   Yes, you did me a great favor. I realize that. I couldn't tell you then because I was so upset. I'm afraid I was somewhat brutish. It was all so unexpected. To hear those sweet words coming through your lips. I felt my heart was being torn to pieces. I suffered as I had never suffered before.

JOSEPHINE: And is that the favor that you have come to thank me for?

ZUBIAGA: It took a great weight off me. But what I've really come for is to ask you to give me the opportunity to speak with her again. (*a gesture from Josephine*) You can't refuse me that comfort. I beg of you. (*Josephine drops her head.*) For a week I haven't been able to sleep because of thinking of her. I keep seeing her just as she was then, sitting at the piano. I hear Mendelssohn's "Spring Song," with its opening bars constantly sounding in my ears. (*softly*) I feel her hands caressing my head. The memory of her has become an obsession. I can't go on enduring such terrible anguish.

JOSEPHINE (*revealing her suffering as she looks at him*) :   Doctor . . . Your words pain me. You don't know how sorry I am for all that happened. But unfortunately what you ask is impossible.

ZUBIAGA (*with a change of tone*): But you don't understand . . .

JOSEPHINE: Yes, I understand your great need for communication again with her. That always happens after the first time. But there is something that might be an obstacle even to my greatest desire to do as you wish. You made the mistake of telling me everything that happened. And your letter made such an impression on me that I am sure it would be impossible to repeat the experience.

ZUBIAGA: It would do no harm to try.

JOSEPHINE: No, doctor. Please don't insist. It's quite impossible. My nerves wouldn't stand it. I failed in the last séance. You know very well that I ended up in bed with a high temperature. I don't believe my nerves could stand another attempt. I'm so tired. I can't stand any more.

ZUBIAGA (*angrily*): Your body can stand anything. You refused to receive me, but you weren't in bed with a fever as you say.

JOSEPHINE: Why, doctor!

ZUBIAGA: You were up and around and perfectly well.

JOSEPHINE: Are you telling me I lied to you?

ZUBIAGA: Absolutely. You went out night before last at 10 P.M.

JOSEPHINE: I assure you I did nothing of the kind.

ZUBIAGA: I saw you. I followed you. You went to the Commissioner. You spent an hour in the Police Station.

JOSEPHINE: You must have confused me with . . .

ZUBIAGA: I even know what you talked about.

JOSEPHINE: You do?

ZUBIAGA: There's a complaint against you by Peluffo, who used to be the mayor, for illegal practices. Today there's an investigator coming from La Plata to arrest you.

JOSEPHINE: You mean, that's what somebody told you.

ZUBIAGA: And that's why you're packing. To run away from here.

JOSEPHINE: No, that's not why I'm leaving.

ZUBIAGA: You're certainly a master at lying.

JOSEPHINE (*sincerely*):   You're right. I confess it. I wasn't ill. That was just an excuse for not seeing you. I didn't feel able to meet you again face to face without blushing for shame. Yet, a few minutes ago when I heard your voice over the phone, I couldn't refuse. . . . It's time to tell you the whole truth. I'm a wretch, Doctor Zubiaga. Out of pride, when I thought I was beaten, to keep you here in town I stooped to a dishonorable trick. I lied, doctor! It's all been a trick, as I say. That séance was a farce. But when I saw how it upset you, I didn't have the strength to go on with it.

ZUBIAGA: Don't look at me like that, with pity in your eyes. I don't need any. You're the one to be pitied. From the beginning, I caught on. I realized the way you were trying to deceive me.

JOSEPHINE (*indignantly*):   You knew? Yet you came here begging me, almost weeping. What kind of monster are you?

ZUBIAGA: I wanted to see how far you'd dare go. Oh, you had details enough to convince anybody. I don't deny that when I left here, I had a moment of uncertainty. It lasted only until I went to Balcarce and learned where you had unearthed all those intimate details, so beautifully embellished. You have an excellent assistant. He's a good psychologist. He knows very well that with a hundred pesos he can buy the goodwill of a talkative old servant. I don't deny it was an artistic performance. You were a second Duse. But to use those details to play on the affection of a sensitive man who had done nothing to you has only one description: infamous!

JOSEPHINE (*imitating him*):   Excellent. Bravo, Barrymore!

What an actor! You knew, and yet you talk about affection. *(with a hysterical laugh)* What a joke! Why, you are a thousand times more infamous and low than I am. There's no word in the dictionary to describe what you've done. You threw yourself at my feet. You wept, you moaned, you let me caress your head. You did a fine job of making me swallow the pill. Scoundrel! Bandit, Ham actor. Tartuffe. No wonder you write plays. But at least I have a reason and an excuse for everything I did. It was out of love. Yes, love. Love for you. A deep love like a flame that you have just extinguished forever with one puff. You've killed it coldly, craftily. The ambitious dramatist wanted to study a character, so he could put me into one of his plays. You made a fool of me to earn your royalties. You're a thousand times more of a scoundrel and wretch than I am, so please get out of my life. Get out of here!

ZUBIAGA: Josephine!

JOSEPHINE: No, don't speak to me. Can't you understand? I never want to see you again. I can never be sorry enough for the love I felt for you. I hate you with all my heart. I'd like to scratch you, strangle you! *(Both her hands are around Zubiaga's throat as he embraces her.)*

ZUBIAGA: Kill me, Josephine! What greater pleasure than to die in your arms? I love you.

JOSEPHINE: Let me go!

ZUBIAGA: I adore you. *(all this rapidly and at the same time)*

JOSEPHINE *(striking his shoulder with her fist)* : Let me go.

ZUBIAGA: I've always loved you.

JOSEPHINE: Liar!

ZUBIAGA: Ever since the first day. I've been mad about you, Josephine.

JOSEPHINE: Let me go or I'll scream. *(Zubiaga shuts her off with his lips on hers. He has his back to the audience.*

Josephine's hand, clenched into a fist, continues pound-
ing on his back. Under the pressure of the kiss, it opens,
and her two arms wind around his neck. She continues
to exclaim) I hate you! I hate you! (*Steps can be heard.*
Josephine releases him and steps back. The back door
opens. Enter Manuel much upset.)

MANUEL: Sister!

JOSEPHINE: What is it?

MANUEL: They're bringing you a baby. She's dying.

JOSEPHINE: Tell them to come in. (*Before she finishes, a*
Mother and Father rush in, the Mother carrying a small
child.)

MOTHER (*desperate and gasping*) :   Sister, she's choking!
Hurry! She's dying. Save her.

JOSEPHINE: Keep calm. Keep calm. (*She and Zubiaga ap-*
proach the child.) How long has she been like this?

MOTHER: It started with a fever.

FATHER: Her throat was sore.

JOSEPHINE: Who looked after her?

MOTHER: Nobody.

ZUBIAGA: It's the croup. She must have an operation. Have
you alcohol? What about a bisturi and scissors? (*Zubi-*
aga has taken off his coat and is turning back his
sleeves. His motions are quick and nervous.)

JOSEPHINE (*stopping him*) :   Just a moment. I'm doing the
operating. In my house you don't touch anybody.

ZUBIAGA: Josephine!

JOSEPHINE: Carry her into the operating room. Hurry.
There's no time to lose. (*The father and mother go*
through the side door left, that Manuel opens. Jose-
phine follows. Zubiaga stands shocked, but reacts
quickly as the door is shut in front of him.)

ZUBIAGA: Why, that woman is out of her mind! She has no
sense of responsibility.

MANUEL: Don't worry! She has done this before and it has
always turned out all right.

ZUBIAGA: But what will she operate with?

MANUEL: A pen knife, doctor.

ZUBIAGA (*frightened*):   She'll kill the baby. I can't allow such a thing. (*Zubiaga rushes to the door and tries the knob, but it is locked from the inside. Mad with anger, he pounds on the door.*) Open up! Open the door, I say. (*He turns to Manuel, who is smiling.*) This is a crime. And to think I just kissed that woman! What am I made of? A doctor, to allow such a thing? What devil spell has she put on me?

MANUEL (*pulling him away from the door*):   Calm yourself, doctor. We've pulled through many crises like this before, and we're still not in jail.

ZUBIAGA: But you will be, soon. (*He rushes to the telephone.*)

MANUEL: What are you going to do? (*Without answering, Zubiaga picks up the receiver. Manuel takes it away, replaces it, and pushes him off.*)

ZUBIAGA: What do you mean by this?

MANUEL: Leave that phone alone.

ZUBIAGA (*threateningly*):   Why, I'll break . . .

MANUEL (*pushing the phone still farther away*):   You're not going to break anything. Don't forget that you're not at home. In the houses of others, you should show good manners. Sit there. (*They look at each other.*) Sit down if you don't want to be put down. (*Zubiaga sits mechanically. Manuel at the phone*) Pancho, The Eagle Pharmacy please. (*to Zubiaga*) Confound it, you try the patience of a saint! Oh, Hello, González. Manuel here. Please send somebody up right away with three ampoules of a thousand units of anti-diphtheria vaccine. From the Pasteur Institute, and hurry it. (*He hangs up. In the silence, Zubiaga stares as if hypnotized.*)

ZUBIAGA: Pasteur Institute? What kind of quack doctors are you?

MANUEL: Don't get upset. Forgive me if I was rude. I'm

sorry. I'm hard to get along with and full of mustard, but you're pure nerves and full of gunpowder. But tell me, young man, do you think that if Sister Josephine hadn't been sure she could cope with it, she'd ever have attempted it? Not even if she had been out of her mind. We know very well what we are doing. (*The door left opens. Enter Josephine wearing a surgeon's gown, its sleeves doubled back. She carries a basin.*)

JOSEPHINE: Well, that's over. (*She crosses the stage to the desk.*)

MANUEL: Successful?

JOSEPHINE (*laying the basin on the desk*): Completely. In a few minutes, take them home. Give the baby the serum when it comes and have some oxygen ready if it should be necessary. (*Exit Manuel to the operating room.*)

ZUBIAGA (*looking into the basin*): Why, this is a tracheotomy canula! (*He lifts it to examine it.*)

JOSEPHINE: Naturally. Did you expect me to use an irrigating tube?

ZUBIAGA (*still looking at the contents of the basin*): And forceps, and bisturi! Josephine, what's the meaning of this? I demand you tell me at once. Manuel said you would be using a penknife instead of a scalpel. (*sounds of voices offstage*)

JOSEPHINE: Just a minute. (*at the door*) What's going on out there?

PANCHO: No, you can't go in!

FIRST DETECTIVE: What do you mean, I can't go in?

SECOND: We're part of the investigating commission.

FIRST: We have court orders.

SECOND: Where is the quack doctor?

JOSEPHINE: (*at the door*): Let them in, Pancho. Come in, gentlemen. What do you want? (*Enter the two Detectives, followed by the Policeman.*)

FIRST DETECTIVE (*to Policeman*): Stand by the door and

don't let anybody leave. (*The Policeman takes his position just as Manuel comes out of the operating room.
The Second Detective looks into the room.*)

SECOND DETECTIVE: What's the matter with the child? (*silence*) Well, answer, somebody!

MANUEL: Sister Josephine operated on her.

FIRST (*looking into the basin*) :   What is this, a butcher
shop?

JOSEPHINE: Would you mind telling me what you want?

SECOND: We've come from La Plata to investigate a complaint of illegal practice of medicine.

JOSEPHINE: All right. You've investigated. I have just operated on a baby that had the croup. I made a cut here
(*gestures*) so that she could breathe. She was purple,
but she's all right now.

ZUBIAGA: Josephine!

SECOND: And you, sir? Who are you?

JOSEPHINE: Don't say anything!

SECOND: What do you mean, Don't say anything?

JOSEPHINE: I just told him not to say anything. You came
to investigate me. Are you going to arrest me? Tell me
why. Because I cure people? If I cure, it's because I
know how to cure. But don't be too pleased with yourselves. Manuel, bring that roll. (*Manuel goes to the
obvious chest and opens it. At that moment, enter the
Chief Investigator, at the rear door.*)

FIRST: (*gesturing toward Josephine*) :   There she is, Mr.
Investigator.

SECOND: We surprised her just as she had operated on a
small child. The patient is still in there.

FIRST (*pointing to the basin*) :   And there are her instru-
ments, sir.

ZUBIAGA: I can't allow this, Josephine.

CHIEF INVESTIGATOR (*who has looked at no one but Josephine since his arrival*) :   Josephine? That's not Josephine. Impossible! You're Sara García.

JOSEPHINE: Yes, doctor.

CHIEF: Do you mean you're the quack doctor? Is this why they dragged me up here from La Plata? Why, you're a better doctor than I am!

MANUEL *(unrolling a diploma that he has taken from the chest)* : You are quite right. Here is her diploma. Full of cobwebs. I'm glad you came so it could be taken out once in a while to air.

ZUBIAGA: Josephine, is that yours?

JOSEPHINE: Yes.

CHIEF: You, the second highest graduate of the class of '29! Winner of the Wilde Prize. But doctor, how could you possibly end up this way?

JOSEPHINE: It's a sad story. When I graduated in 1929 I thought like all the new doctors, that with a diploma it would be easy to earn a living. Full of optimism, I hung out my shingle in Buenos Aires, Corner of Sarmiento and Suipacha. A good office. But in the next six months I saw only two patients.

MANUEL: One with a cut finger and one with a cold.

JOSEPHINE: That's right, Manuel. Don't you know who Manuel is? He was the laboratory assistant at Medical School. During my anatomy examination he helped me locate an appendix. Indicated it with the forceps.

MANUEL: She got a perfect 10 on her record.

JOSEPHINE: We signed an agreement that day to start together, and we've kept it, "There are too many doctors in Buenos Aires," Manuel said one day: "Let's go into the country." So we did, looking at one small town after another but finding no community willing to make use of what I had learned of medicine. Then one day Manuel said: "Why is it that quack doctors get rich while regular doctors die of hunger?" That's the day my new life began. To face it, I threw into the chest as useless ballast the diploma that had cost me so much sacrifice and hard work. I became a quack doctor. Immediately suffering humanity trusted me and flocked to my door. And since I had been taught how to cure them, success and fortune followed. Now I'm retiring, gentlemen. I've saved enough to live on till regular patients begin coming to me. And that's my story. (*Manuel, who has rolled up the diploma and tossed it into the chest, lets the cover fall with a bang.*)

CHIEF: Very interesting. Well, with your permission. There's nothing for us but to leave. (*He bows.*) Madame doctor!

JOSEPHINE (*bowing to him*): Doctor! (*The two detectives also bow and leave. Manuel remains, facing Josephine and Zubiaga. Manuel looks sad.*)

MANUEL: That is the end of our agreement.

JOSEPHINE: Why, Manuel?

MANUEL (*gesturing to the two of them*): Well, can't you see? Besides, you've achieved your economic independence. I . . .

JOSEPHINE: So have you, Manuel. You will become mayor. I can get you elected mayor.

MANUEL: I know.

JOSEPHINE: There's lots of good you can still do.

MANUEL: I'll try. (*much moved*) Whatever happens, señorita, I'll never forget you.

JOSEPHINE: Nor shall I.

MANUEL: With your permission, since I know I am not needed here . . . (*He brushes his eyes with his hand as he goes out.*)

ZUBIAGA: Forgive me! I'm so ashamed. I've been an imbecile. Twice an imbecile. For not realizing you must be a doctor and for being too blind to see I loved you. Sara, I adore you! (*He takes her in his arms.*)

JOSEPHINE (*putting her finger on his lips*): No, not Sara. Josephine.

ZUBIAGA: Josephine. (*He kisses her.*)

CURTAIN

The Fate of Chipí González

A MODERN MIRACLE PLAY IN THREE ACTS

CHARACTERS

Saul, *an angel*

Mom, *a devil*

Chipí (Cipriano González)
a football player

Pedro, *his father*

Conche, *his mother*

Don Luis Benítez

Anastacio (Anastá)
a football booster

Ramón, *a boyhood friend*

Lola, *whom Chipí loves*

Marta Benítez,
who loves Chipí

Justice of Peace

Four football fans (two with speaking parts)

*The same set for all three acts: the front yard of
a Paraguayan farm near a small village*

ACT 1

Scene 1 — Morning

As the curtain rises, the stage is dark. A spotlight casts its light on the drops that represent the firmament with its clouds. Saul slowly enters into its radiance. Within the clouds are lights illuminating the two actors from below, leaving the lower part of the stage in darkness. As the cloud illumination increases, the spotlight is extinguished.

Saul is an angel, as beautiful and as pure as the face of the actor and the make-up man permit. Blond hair falls over his shoulders. He wears a white robe, caught at the waist by a white cord. He has no wings because that would involve theological argument; but on his head rests a golden halo, something allowed any aspirant to holiness. He has the air of pathetic boredom; to be immortal and bored are enough to encourage suicide.

SAUL: What horrible boredom! The only justification of eternity is the contemplation of God, to be in the divine presence. But when the Lord permits us to wander through the universe, even an angel feels oppressed by the monotony of these immense spaces where suns spin about and constellations of dead stars emerge and pass, shadowless, like black, coagulated masses of forgetfulness.

(Enter Mom. He stands behind Saul, smiling. He is one of the ordinary sort of devils that wander about by thousands. His hair is short for hygienic reasons and to keep cool. He wears two blunt horns coquettishly

56

planted among his curls. He also wears a tunic, because he has discovered it is a comfortable garment. But it is grey, so as not to show dirt. In his country, water is scarce, and laundry prices are high.)

SAUL: Sometimes I'm a bit envious of my brothers who in the Age of Genesis could descend to earth and love the fair daughters of man. It was an abasement, undoubtedly, but an angel could purify himself later, and so could better understand the worth of eternal glory.

MOM: You are ill, Saul! You need problems.

SAUL *(without surprise)*:   Oh, it's you, Mom? Cure my boredom with some ingenious temptation, won't you?

MOM: So that's the trouble? *(sadly)* I'm sorry I can't help you. I'm only a bureaucrat in the Public Administration of Hell. I've even lost the last traces of my old wings. My time is spent making out lists. The same dull work for centuries! *(Sighs.)* I'm not a devil any longer; I'm hardly a poor devil.

SAUL: Where I live, we have no bureaucracy.

MOM: I know. On account of the few souls you get, you've got room to let them wander wherever they want, through the valleys, villages, and flowery fields. An enchanting idyll! But we get so many souls that we have a terrific problem of organization.

SAUL: Well, why don't you cut down on your devices to tempt mortals?

MOM: Don't make me laugh! Centuries ago we gave up tempting mortals. All of us authentic devils live like slaves just writing regulations, finding places for the crowds, stopping the fights, trying to change the habits of the damned souls, to make them submissive and orderly, so they can all live together in Hell. *(He shrugs his shoulders.)* Nowadays, men tempt themselves and condemn themselves, and yet, look at the numbers of them!

(Though only the cloud is illuminated, and the lower part of the stage is dark, yet one can distinguish the forms of people, though not any individuals. From the right, enters a file of a dozen people, fastened to one another by a single cord that passed around their necks. Their hands are behind them, as if tied, and they shuffle along as though burdened by a heavy weight. Their pace is rhythmical, as they cross the stage and exeunt left.)

SAUL: Yes, that's the way they look from Eternity.

MOM: The eternal mystery oppresses them!

(The same line comes back, linked by the same cord, but now they sway like dancers. A soft and far-off melody is heard, and the line raises its arms to heaven in fervent entreaty. Their movements are choreographic, though it is impossible to distinguish any of them. They go out right, and the music dies away.)

SAUL *(smiling tenderly)* : Now they are dreaming.

MOM: Maybe, but awake or dreaming, they have a savage pride. They are sure they can transform and master the whole of creation. That's what brings them in hordes to our region.

SAUL: Wouldn't you like to enjoy yourself watching them a little while at close range?

MOM *(shrugging his shoulders to indicate indifference)* : All right, I haven't anything else to do. It's my vacation, you know.

SAUL: Well, God grant it relieves my boredom. I'll make an effort and enter into Time.

(The light in the cloud is extinguished. The stage is illuminated. On the spectator's right is a small Paraguayan farm house with an open porch in the front, with low base walls around it to keep out the rain. In the rear, is the wall of the farm house, with a practical

door. *The backdrop allows one to go behind the house.
It has a painted tree under which are scattered tools,
wheels, tires, etc. To the left is evidence of vegetation
with the horizon indicated, above which is suspended
the cloud.*

*From the beams of the porch hang tobacco leaves to
dry, clusters of corn, and tools. A kettle and stove under
the roof. Outside, a cot covered with leather-hide under
a mosquito netting framework. Several rustic benches
and some homemade chairs of tree branches. Enter
Luis, a man getting along in years. He wears a coarse
straw hat with chin strap, a linen shirt, white cotton
trousers, a wide belt, and sandals.*)

LUIS *(loudly)* :   Good morning! Where's my old friend?

PEDRO *(from behind the house)* :   Is that you, Luis? Come
in. Sit down. I'll be with you in a minute!

LUIS *(sitting)* :   What are you doing, Old Man?

*(Enter Pedro, right, from behind the house. He is about
fifty, with white hair, but still vigorous. He is barefoot
with his cotton trousers turned up, halfway to his knees.
Wears a coarse straw hat with chin strap, and old-fashioned oval spectacles, with silver frames.)*

PEDRO: I was fixing the eaves. When I went looking for a
file, I noticed that the wind last night had blown off
some of the thatch.

LUIS: Any harm done?

PEDRO: No. *(Goes to the stove to get the horn cup in which
yerba maté is brewed, and some water for the maté.)*
The rain was certainly welcome. The plow sinks in, this
morning, and the earth has a good smell. The new
moon came up full of water and it looks like we'll get
more rain this month.

LUIS: Yes, I agree with you.

PEDRO: I'm plowing for cotton this year. They say it'll
bring good money.

LUIS: That's what they always say, but when you get paid, your money isn't worth anything.

PEDRO: That's right. The middlemen get all the profit.

LUIS: Then they send somebody to pay us and the only money he pays out is in words.

PEDRO: That's the way it goes. But I'm getting old, friend. Just so I get all the food I need—my heart's kicking up on me. (*Sighs.*) Sometimes that good-for-nothing ticker thumps inside me like a galloping horse.

LUIS: What do you take, friend?

PEDRO: Elderberry and thorn rose tea, with grass roots in the maté.

LUIS: That's pretty good, but I had an attack the other day and rue brought me around. Why don't you try some in your tea?

PEDRO: All right, I'll get some.

LUIS (*confidentially*):   And put a little furze in the maté, too.

PEDRO: What for?

LUIS: That's strong stuff. (*with a leer.*) You'll get along fine with the old lady, then.

PEDRO: Really?

LUIS: You bet. It used to be I'd think no more about mine than I would about an old cow—but since I've used what I told you in the maté, I see an old cow and think about the missus.

(*The two old reprobates chuckle. Pedro is about to ask further questions, when enter Conche right, with a bundle on her head. She is a woman of about forty, but looks older. Though shrunken, she is strong. Her eyes are red and her skin is stained by the smoke of the oven. Her long hair contains a couple of white pins, but hangs in two scanty pigtails. Her costume is a square-necked shirtwaist and faded skirt hanging to the middle of her shins. She is barefoot, and in the hand that she swings to balance the bundle is a worn machete.*)

CONCHE: The manioc is growing fine. It's a pleasure to work the ground today.

PEDRO: What about Chipí? Didn't he come back with you?

CONCHE: He left early for the Kola farm. I haven't seen him since then.

PEDRO: That boy! (*He shakes his head.*) He's completely crazy about soccer football. On Mondays he can't work because he's got to boast about what happened in the game Sunday. And Tuesdays he starts practice again. And Wednesdays—

CONCHE: Heavens, Pedro! It's not as bad as that. Besides, it's more better to play football than cards.

LUIS: Maybe better, but football is driving us crazy these days. My daughter Marta has a new dress that she won't wear because it has the colors of the "Presidente" team. She wants to sell it. She'll be wanting to wear football shoes to a dance one of these days.

PEDRO: The boy looks on his playing as work, and looks on work— (*hesitating*) —well, as work.

LUIS (*Laughs, and then sighs.*):   That's true, old man. Our youth, the hope of the country, thinks only of football, while we old folk—we couldn't see a goal post even with glasses.

CONCHE (*angrily*):   Shut up! You two used to go in for lots worse kinds of sport, and you still do! (*Confronting them.*) I know both of you very well, I do! A fine pair of rascals! (*Pedro and Luis look at each other surprised and with a gesture of "The very idea!" But when Conche turns away, they can't hold back their satisfied snickers.*)

(*Enter Chipí and Lola, left, holding hands. Chipí is a young man of twenty, tanned and strong. He wears a football jersey, cotton trousers, and sneakers. Lola is a blonde with green-gold eyes, and light chestnut hair, tied back with a ribbon. She has a slim, graceful body with the daring coquetry of country girls who lack self-possession. A printed skirt and tight white shirt-waist that accentuates her bust. She wears hemp-soled shoes.)*

CHIPÍ *(with straw hat in his hand)* :   Good morning, father. *(He seeks a blessing.)*

LOLA: Good morning. *(Luis answers her. The others are listening to the conversation between Chipi and his father.)*

PEDRO *(Nods at Lola, then raises his hand and repeats the blessing formula between his teeth.)* :   God bless you! *(then without pause and with evident ill humor)* Where was you all morning?

CHIPÍ: When I got up, I went looking for the ox that was missing, on account of last night's storm.

PEDRO *(ironically)* :   I suppose the wind blew him far away.

CHIPÍ: Well, I went as far as the irrigation ditch and then in the distance I saw some animals. I went to look, but he wasn't among them. When I got back, I saw him beside the road, near a haystack. I must have gone past without seeing him.

PEDRO: You mean your mind was on your football! Is that all you did?

CHIPÍ: Well, after that, while I was jumping the ditch beside the Kola fence, I fell and hurt my leg. *(He pulls up the left trouser leg, but there is not the slightest sign of a wound.)* And so I stopped to see the trainer and get a massage.

CONCHE: Did you hurt yourself very much, my son?

PEDRO *(looking at the leg and touching it)* :   Poor fellow! And where is this mortal wound?

CHIPÍ: You can't see anything, but the trainer says there's a

muscle separation in my calf: and I'll realize it as soon
as I kick very hard.

PEDRO: Dear me! How terrible! Maybe a little Paraguayan
gymnastics would be good for you. Just go and work out
in the manioc field, my boy. You'll feel better after
weeding three or four rows. It's a sure remedy.

LOLA: But, Mr. González! The trainer gave him a rubdown
with rum. He's got to rest. There's a game with the
Twenty-Two club on Sunday, and they're bringing a
band and everything.

PEDRO: And the game with the soup kettle comes every day
at twelve and the poor boy has to take part in that, too.

CONCHE: How can he work if he's hurt? You sit around
mixing your yerba maté, and sucking your maté, and
expect a person who's hurt is going to work! Fine!

*(Pedro shrugs and, looking at Luis, says, "You see!"
Luis nods hopelessly. Lola and Conche help Chipi to sit
on the cot. He limps but endures the pain with injured
pride.)*

CONCHE: Lie down, my boy! *(Lola lifts the injured leg. He
sighs when she takes off his shoe.)* Shall I rub it with
candle grease? Gently?

CHIPÍ *(still insulted)* :   Leave me alone, Mama.

LOLA: I'm going to rub it whether he wants or not.

CHIPÍ *(shrugging his shoulders in disgust)* :   It's all right.

LOLA: Keep quiet; don't be stubborn!

*(As she takes off his shoe—he does not wear socks—
Chipi has an uncontrollable desire to stretch his peasant
feet, imprisoned in a shoe. He takes advantage of the
time Lola is not looking to separate the toes, and his
face shows his keen pleasure.)*

LOLA: Where does it hurt?

CHIPÍ: A little higher up—oh—ouch! Down lower! *(under
his breath, to her)* You've got gentle hands, you beautiful blonde!

LUIS: Well, friend, I've got to be going. I wanted to ask you to lend me your ox on Thursday. My old "red-and-white" is hard to manage.

(*Conche brings a candle stub and tries to soften it between her fingers. She gives it to Lola. They discuss in low voices what ought to be done. Conche goes back to her chores and the young ones are lost in a murmured conversation.*)

PEDRO: Well, what do you think? Shall we send for the trainer to give him a massage?

LUIS: Ha, ha! Seems to me he ate some poison herbs.

PEDRO: Maybe he ate some of that "good stuff" that you recommended to me, and he's thinking about some of his binges. (*The two laugh with a certain cynicism that covers their melancholy.*) Sure, early Thursday I'll send the ox with Chipí (*looking with amusement at the boy*) if he's not too busy with his practicing. (*Chipí turns his head on hearing his name. When Luis gets up to shake hands with Pedro, the lights go out on the lower stage and there is illumination again on the cloud. The action continues below in the darkness till the people blend with the deep shadows and disappear.*)

MOM: Not much action in this spectacle, Saul.

SAUL: Don't worry! This is no backwoods. Things will start moving.

MOM (*with bad humor*): I suppose so, because this fellow they call Cipriano González, alias Chipí, is going to end up in Hell.

SAUL (*astonished*): How can you know that Chipí will go to Hell if you devils can't foresee the future? Don't you have to let things develop till time for the punishment?

MOM: It's true we can't see into the future, but the vast number of lost souls, the lack of capacity of our plant, and the urgent need for expansion have forced us to inaugurate a system of technical studies to forecast the number of souls that we shall receive in any given period.

SAUL: And your technical studies can predict the destiny of each individual?

MOM: With remarkable accuracy. Our Statistical Institute of Probabilities is so scientifically organized that when a soul comes into the world, from an investigation of its genetic antecedents, with data on its education and information on its surroundings, we can put together everything into a final formula when it reaches puberty, and we can tell whether to heat up the furnaces, or expect it to go elsewhere.

SAUL: Diabolical! Diabolical! I'd never have thought—! So Chipí González is damned?

MOM: He's on our list, and I can see from here the location of the furnace planned for him.

SAUL: What a pity! Poor damned Chipí González! Do you know, I've got a kindly feeling for him. I'm sorry that I, who am outside of Time, can't ever know his final destiny, as you will.

MOM: What is your point of view toward the mortals on earth?

SAUL (*meditating*): At first we see them as they look from a great distance away. Since for us there's no past, present, or future, the mass can't be distinguished and doesn't move. It's just millions of small lights, close together, burning and going out on an infinitely large plain. Only by a great effort of the mind do I sometimes enter into a few of them and see their lives, for a moment, as I'm doing now.

MOM: Can't you follow the destiny of one man from his birth to the death that will come to him eventually?

SAUL: Human life is so feeble and ephemeral that I can't follow the journey of just one man. It would be the same as stirring up an ant hill and trying to keep an eye on just one ant. They're all scrambled. (*Thinks.*) I do, however, have one way.

MOM: What's that?

SAUL: There is something more stable than the life of a man.

MOM: I don't understand.

SAUL: I mean his tracks, the documents about his passage through the earth.

MOM: But he leaves those tracks as he goes along. How could you have documents that deal with his future?

SAUL: Very simple! Since Time does not exist for me, I can lay my hands on documents still in the future.

MOM: It sounds complicated. What documents, for instance, do you have about the future of Chipí González?

SAUL (*concentrating*): Chipí González! (*He lowers his left hand and without looking at what he is doing, he lifts up a letter.*) Here is a letter from the National Football Club of Asunción. It offers a bonus of seven thousand guaraníes for Chipí. So, applying a little logic, I deduce that he is going to be a football star.

MOM: Anything else?

SAUL (*the same pantomine and he raises another paper*): This confirms it. A little while later, he'll be playing on his local team for the League Championship. Here's the program of the game: Date, championship, etc.

MOM: Do they win the game?

SAUL (*same pantomime. He raises a trophy cup.*): Yes, they will win. Here's the club's name engraved as champions for the year.

MOM: What else?

SAUL (*Lifts a register of a Justice of the Peace*): The day of the game he'll get married. Here is the marriage certificate, in legal form. Applying reason, it's quite evident that they will celebrate the championship and the marriage with a big party and Chipí will go with his wife to the city to play football according to his contract. (*He stops and meditates.*) Now I understand. I'm sure that he'll fall prey to greed and vanity, and end by going down with you.

MOM: Aren't there any other documents?

SAUL (*Seeks again, then shakes his head*): No, nothing more. About the rest of his life, I know nothing.

MOM (*after a pause*):   I'd like to know what happens to him.

SAUL: Well, let's take a look, then. (*They peer over the edge of the cloud. At this moment, on the darkened stage below, is heard a roar like a hurricane and people running about—the distant cry of a woman for help, the oaths of some men, rifle fire, and the far-off sound of a cannon shot.*)

MOM: The devil! While we've been talking, they've had a revolution!

SAUL: Time isn't the same for us as for them down there. (*All the lights go out.*)

CURTAIN

Scene 2

As the curtain goes up, six months have passed since the end of the first scene. Now, no food is hanging from the beams of Pedro's porch. His clothes and Conche's are torn and dirty. With a mallet, Conche is smashing coconuts to extract the meat, which, in these evil times, is the only thing they have to eat.

PEDRO (*coming out through the door*):   Is there a bit of yerba maté, Conche?

CONCHE: You'll find a little of the new leaves to mix with the leaves that are drying.

PEDRO (*sighing*) :   If that's all we got, where is it? (*pause*)
Luis won't give me back my ox.

CONCHE (*Gestures with her head toward a board on which
the leaves are drying.*) :   There they are! (*She points to
an almost empty bag hanging from a beam of the
eaves.*) And there's what's left. (*She goes back to her
tasks.*) They've got to give him back to you.

PEDRO (*Takes down the horn maté cup and the perforated
tube through which it is sucked. He grabs a handful of
used maté, and then squeezes the pouch to get out what
is left in it.*) :   I suppose, unless they slaughter him.

CONCHE: Why would they slaughter the ox? Won't he be
worth more if they make him work?

PEDRO: No. (*settling the yerba inside the horn container,
around the tube*) Because they're afraid.

CONCHE (*stopping her work*) :   Afraid? Why?

PEDRO: That they'll have to give him back to me.

CONCHE (*opening coconuts again*) :   I don't know what you
mean.

PEDRO: When you're not a regular robber, Justice enters
here inside you, and shouts: "You're a thief!" You're
frightened; you want to run away, but where are you
going to go if you're here? (*tapping his chest*) So you
throw away or kill what you stole.

CONCHE: And keep quiet?

PEDRO: I don't know. But you throw away or kill on account of fear, fear that's inside you.

CONCHE: And then the feeling goes away?

PEDRO: No, but that's all you can do. It's like death. And
when there's no help for it, it's easier to forget it.

CONCHE (*sighing*) :   It ought not to be. (*She stops pounding
and sinks to her knees.*) Holy Mary forbid!

PEDRO: Never mind, Conche. Don't worry. (*He serves himself maté and looks into the distance.*) Nobody dies
before his time. We're a couple of tough old people who

can stand anything. We either die or can live through anything. *(He gets up and puts his hand on Conche's head.)* Are you going to die?

CONCHE *(Straightens up, surprised.)* :   No!

PEDRO: Then we'll live through it. *(He laughs at his joke.)* Ha, ha! Well, guess I'll go see if Tomás has a little maté to take to Chipí tomorrow. *(Starts out, right.)*

CONCHE *(without looking up)* :   Don't bother, Pedro! I saved some for him.

PEDRO *(facing her)* :   You did, eh? And made me use the green stuff?

CONCHE *(defiantly)* :   He's hiding in the brush. But at least he's still there, though many have gone away. I don't want him to go, too. *(imploring)* Don't let him go!

PEDRO: Where?

CONCHE: To some other mountain, or other valley. Where he can find friends. Where they haven't forgotten that we're all neighbors.

(Enter Luis, left. His improved social status is shown by his boots, riding trousers, pajama coat, and felt hat. A revolver hangs at his belt, and he carries a heavy riding whip in his left hand. He does not remove his hat.)

LUIS: How are you getting along around here? *(Slaps his boot with his whip in impatient insolence.)*

PEDRO *(humbly)* :   Pretty well. Sit down, Luis—I mean, Mr. Commissioner. *(He brushes off a bench on which Luis sits pompously.)* What would you like, Mr. Commissioner? *(Conche mutters a greeting and goes on with her task.)*

LUIS: I've come for the last time to discuss that bum called Chipí, the one you are hiding.

CONCHE: He's not here. We've told you that, Mr. Commissioner.

LUIS: So you keep on denying it? The police believe he's

one of that gang of cattle thieves living in the mountain.

PEDRO: That's not true, Commissioner. He's no thief.

CONCHE: If there are any cattle thieves around here, it's you! Everybody knows that. And knows that you blame somebody else.

PEDRO (*approaching her, alarmed, trying to calm her*): Hush, Conche.

LUIS (*jumping up indignantly and talking at the same time as Pedro*): I won't permit you loose-tongued women to insult the government and its authority. The idea! That's what comes of being soft with you people. (*pointing with his whip*) It doesn't do you any good to get touchy, Miss' Conche. (*to Pedro*) And you! She's your responsibility. Shut her up or I'll put you in jail, incommunicado, as an example!

PEDRO: But, old friend—

LUIS (*violently*): Don't call me "old friend" when I'm in the government. You've got into bad habits. People have been too easy-going with you. But I didn't come here just to chat. Either surrender your son, Chipí, or make good the oxen he stole.

CONCHE: Take our oxen, Mr. Commissioner! They're yours. We're working just for you. Take them, Mr. Commissioner.

(*Saul and Mom take part in the scene, invisible to the others who go on without noticing them as they come in, right, down stage.*)

MOM: Did you see that? His old friend, his pal, now that he has a bureaucratic job, acts like an overbearing petty boss!

SAUL: And how he enjoys it! He, his father, and his grandfather have endured innumerable commissioners, and this is the only revenge they have, to overturn the government and become commissioners themselves.

(Exeunt left, down stage. Meantime Ramón and Anas-
tacio come in, right, from behind the house. Ramón is
about twenty-five and wears a football jersey, the same
color as Chipí's in the first scene. A straw hat and old
cotton trousers, shiny in the seat. Anastacio is a rural
dandy. He wears a white suit, but no necktie or hat.)

ANASTACIO: Good evening. How are you all? How are you,
Mr. Commissioner?

RAMÓN *(at the same time)*:   Good evening. How are we,
Miss' Conche?

PEDRO: Evening. Come in. Take seats. *(He gestures toward*
a bench, but Ramón sits on the cot, and takes out a ball
with a hole in one side, and a stick. He swings the ball
and tries to impale it on the stick.)

CONCHE: We're fine. Sit down, won't you?

ANASTACIO: We've been looking for you everywhere, Mr.
Commissioner. We need you bad.

LUIS: Me? What for? What's the matter?

ANASTACIO *(who had sat down, now gets up and adopts the*
solemn pose of an orator):   Yes, it happens that only
you can be the savior of our football club. Our club, the
glorious 14th of July, needs you. And by unanimous
decision of its members, my friend Ramón and I have
come to offer you the presidency of the Directorial
Committee for the coming season.

LUIS *(visibly flattered)*:   Hum! But my position, the responsibilities of my office, would hardly permit me—
with all these bandits around here—

ANASTACIO: We realize, Mr. Commissioner, that your grave
responsibilities leave you very little time, but we've
come to beg you to make the sacrifice. We are confident
that under your energetic and dynamic leadership, our
club will rise like a lion and fill with glory the playing
fields of Paraguay.

LUIS (*somewhat uneasy*) : But—why do you want to get rid of Amado Minetti?

RAMÓN (*who has also risen when Anastacio began his speech. Aside*) : His money gave out!

ANASTACIO: Amado Minetti requested and deserves a rest. For many years he has had various duties in our glorious committee of directors. He has been a veritable father to our players. He has found work so they could keep in condition. He has helped them financially in periods of crisis, so that they could play without worries. He has entertained them in his house, feeding them to raise their spirits and even slipping a guaraní into their pockets occasionally to let them have a good time with their sweethearts. And after the games, there's always been bottles in his house for the celebrations, and on those days nobody paid except him.

RAMÓN (*aside*) : And so he had to sell all his cattle. (*to the group*) He was a fine sportsman.

LUIS (*seriously*) : You don't seem to need a president. A good cow will do the job, I'm sure.

ANASTACIO: Oh, no, no, Mr. Commissioner! In these times of political disturbance, we need above all a president with an iron hand to keep the players together, to exercise military discipline so they can face their opponents gloriously.

LUIS: Yes, that's so. I'm very energetic, especially when I have responsibilities. When is the meeting?

ANASTACIO: Sunday after the races, Mr. Commissioner.

LUIS: And (*not wishing to ask or knowing how*) is there no other candidate?

ANASTACIO (*casually*) : Oh, yes. Some want to nominate Dr. Cardozo. (*scornfully*) But what good would he be?

RAMÓN: What chance would he have with you, my dear Commissioner? We don't waste any thoughts on him.

(*Conche gets up quietly and lights a lantern which she hangs from a beam in the porch.*)

LUIS: Well, you must consider that sort of people. They're very crafty.

RAMÓN: Yes, but you know (*significantly*), Mr. Commissioner . . .

LUIS: What do you think about having him jailed for a while, as an example?

ANASTACIO: Oh, no! That wouldn't work, Mr. Commissioner! We must proceed democratically. Why, if people like him should win—I won't say anything more.

LUIS: Of course, if we're sure of winning, it's better to do it democratically, but you know, Anastá, with these ignorant people, who have no public instruction, sometimes you can't—

ANASTACIO: Yes, you can't teach them democracy by kindness.

LUIS: That's true. That's why you've got to make them understand with an iron hand.

RAMÓN: Oh, dear Commissioner, how lucky I am to be on your side!

LUIS: Why, my boy, why?

RAMÓN: Because I like democracy, too.

LUIS: For me, democracy comes first, and if there isn't democracy, I don't want to have anything to do with it.

ANASTACIO: Well, Mr. Commissioner, then—I'm asking you, then—can we count on your acceptance?

LUIS: Very well. For the sake of the people, we'll accept this grave responsibility.

(*Anastacio approaches to shake his hand effusively, while Ramón leaps on the bench enthusiastically.*)

RAMÓN: Three cheers for the Commissioner, don Luis Benítez, the future president of the glorious 14th of July Team. Hip Hip— (*Anastacio is the only one who replies. Pedro can't help making a mimic sign of embarrassment each time the opportunity comes.*) Hurray, Hurray! (*Ramón also shakes his hand.*) Hurray!

ANASTACIO: Very well, then, Mr. Commissioner. Now I'll go and tell the rest of the team about the glorious results of our effort. They are waiting for us at the "Drop In" Bar.

LUIS: Let's all go. I'll accompany you. (*He tries to recapture his bureaucratic air, though he cannot conceal his feeling of pleasure.*) And you, Pedro, don't forget what I told you.

PEDRO (*resigned*): Very well, Mr. Commissioner.

ANASTACIO: See you tomorrow, González! (*a nod to Conche*)

PEDRO and CONCHE: Good night. (*Exeunt Luis, Anastacio and Ramón left, talking excitedly. Pedro gets up and puts his poncho on the cot and prepares for bed. He moves slowly, while he talks.*)

PEDRO: Who could have guessed it? (*Shakes his head.*) Grow old, with nothing left but death, a lonely death.

CONCHE (*She has taken an ear of roasted corn and a handful of almonds on a tin plate, but on hearing his words, she turns to him, without putting down what she has in her hand.*): What makes you think you're alone, old man?

PEDRO: I wasn't talking about you, Conche. You and I are one, "The same flesh and blood." I don't know what life would be without you. I meant that when you get older and older, there are many things that die before you do. (*He sits on the cot.*)

CONCHE: Like what?

PEDRO: Many things you used to like. A friend betrays you and is dead as far as you're concerned. Another comes; he seems all right, but you've lost faith. You don't accept him, and you get more and more lonely. You're getting closer to death, alone.

CONCHE (*passionately*): But there's one who will never leave you.

PEDRO: Who's that?

CONCHE: God!

PEDRO (*smiling bitterly*) :   That's the last name for hope!

CONCHE: Don't say that, Pedro! God never leaves you lonely.

(*Enter Ramón rapidly from the left, with an appearance of secret mischief.*)

RAMÓN: Don Pedro—listen a minute!

PEDRO: What's the matter?

RAMÓN (*gesturing to Conche to come closer*) :   Chipí'll be back soon!

CONCHE: Oh, no! Don't let him. (*Looks around in fear.*) They'll grab him if he shows up here.

RAMÓN: No, they won't. Luis himself will go and get him.

PEDRO (*alarmed*) :   You mean they're sending out a search party?

RAMÓN: Oh, no! Nothing like that! Don't worry. What I mean is that Chipí will be back here with safe conduct, to work, to play football, to stay with you.

CONCHE: Why? Who told you?

RAMÓN (*winking broadly*) :   I'm a fixer, I am. Anastacio and I fixed it. Don Luis is going to be the president of our team.

PEDRO: What does that have to do with it?

RAMÓN: Don't you realize that Chipí is the best center forward in the League?

CONCHE: And do you think that he'll get a safe conduct to leave the mountain, just for that?

RAMÓN: Of course! You'll see. I'm going after him in the morning. See you tomorrow. (*Exit left, still talking.*)

Pedro: See you tomorrow.

CONCHE: Thank you, Ramón.

(*Pedro and Conche look at each other seriously. Both are thinking of the coincidence of the blasphemy and the good news, but neither mentions it. Then, Conche lies on the bed, while Pedro blows out the lantern. And the stage is dark. Meantime Saul and Mom enter left, just as Pedro is going to bed. They cross the stage and exeunt right. A dog barks and howls.)*

CONCHE: What makes that dog bark like that?

(Pedro gets up, picks up an ember of wood from the fire and waves it to get it burning, to light up the place.)

PEDRO: Blackie! Blackie! *(Stares into the darkness.)* I don't see anything. *(The dog howls, and then stops barking. Pedro returns with the firebrand and tosses it onto the fire. Then he sits on his cot.)*

CONCHE: I wonder what that was!

PEDRO *(seriously)* :   I don't know. I don't know. There are some things we never know. *(Meditates.)* In the name of the Father, the Son, and the Holy Ghost! *(He crosses himself.)*

CURTAIN

ACT 2
Scene 1 — Morning

When the curtain rises, Anastacio is sitting in a chair and using a bench for a writing desk. Chipi, dressed as he was in the first act, straddles the bench and looks intrigued at what the other is doing. He has a bottle of ink and an envelope.

ANASTACIO *(writing a letter. Solemnly)* :   "Esteemed señorita."

CHIPí: Oh, no, no! That's no good.

ANASTACIO *(with a sarcastic smile)* :   What do you want, then? "My dear señorita."

CHIPí: No, I don't like that. It's not sweet. It's like "esteemed señorita." What do they say in poetry: "Beloved, adored, idolized Lola." *(with a gesture of impa-*

tience) I told you to bring your book of model love letters.

ANASTACIO: But, Chipí, I told you, that book belongs to Lola.

CHIPÍ: Do you think she remembers everything in it?

ANASTACIO: Of course. Women memorize that sort of thing.

CHIPÍ: Oh, I'll bet!

ANASTACIO: They do. And then they laugh because they know where you copied all your sweet words.

CHIPÍ (*nods surprised*) : You know an awful lot, Anastá.

ANASTACIO: As a public accountant—

CHIPÍ (*respectfully*) : I know that. But how shall we start the letter?

ANASTACIO: Well, if you want it sweeter, why not put: "My adored Lola."

CHIPÍ: Yes, that's good. (*Stretches to see what the other is writing.*)

ANASTACIO: "I hope that on receipt of this, you are in a good state of health." (*Chipi starts more gestures of disapproval, but stops.*) "As I am well."

CHIPÍ: That's not sweet, friend. That's not sweet. (*Opens his arms and looks around as though begging aid.*)

ANASTACIO: Wait a minute! Now comes: (*Begins to write.*) —"My heart bleeds for your absence" (*Chipi's face lights up.*) "like—like—" What bleeds a lot?

CHIPÍ (*anxious to help*) : A cow when the butcher—

ANASTACIO (*scornfully*) : Bah! How could I put "my heart bleeds for your absence like a slaughtered cow?"

CHIPÍ: How about a calf?

ANASTACIO: No, wait a minute!

CHIPÍ: Like a bull?

ANASTACIO (*waving him off with his hand, writes with real satisfaction*) : "Like an animal on the altar of sacrifice."

CHIPÍ (*applauding, charmed*) : Oh, my dear Public Accountant, formidable!

ANASTACIO (*continuing to write*) : "I miss you so much, my lovely blonde. I long to see you, even for an instant."

CHIPÍ (*repeats with deep feeling*) : "Even for an instant."

ANASTACIO (*writing*) : "And when I awaken, because in my dreams you are always near—"

CHIPÍ: That's the truth!

ANASTACIO: "When are you coming back, my lovely blonde?"

CHIPÍ: Beautiful!

ANASTACIO: "I must see you. I love you more than (*Hesitates.*) —more than the team."

CHIPÍ: Colossal!

ANASTACIO: No, she won't believe that!

CHIPÍ: Sure. Put it in!

ANASTACIO: "Send me back word, by the truck driver, Mario, when you're coming. Be sure—to answer as soon as—this reaches you. And I take leave of you—with all my love."

CHIPÍ: Love? Love? That's fine!

ANASTACIO: All right—sign it, and that's that.

CHIPÍ: But it's so short! There were so many things I wanted to say.

ANASTACIO: What else? (*Ticks them off on his fingers.*) You told her you loved her. You said you missed her. You said you wanted to see her. You said you dreamed about her. That's all you need in a good love letter.

CHIPÍ (*Bows his head; then, as if talking to himself*) : I wanted to tell her not to forget this valley, tell her to remember the path to the brook, and the morning when I was up a tree eating guayaba, and saw how pretty she was and all the guayaba seeds went inside me and tickled my heart. And remind her of the gate where I used to wait for her, patting my dog and playing the mouth organ to help me think of all the sweet things that I wanted to tell her. Those trees are still here and the same birds still fly around, and don't leave the valley. The same calm night and the stars are all still here, but they seem sad, crying for her because she's left the valley.

ANASTACIO (*who has been staring at him, astonished at the sentiment that came out spontaneously*) :   Very well. Leave that to me. I'll make it a bit more flowery. (*He starts to write as Chipi looks on enthusiastically. Then he stops and hesitates. Chipi straightens up, also disconcerted. There is a pantomime showing the wearing labor of Anastacio and the anxiety of Chipi. Enter Ramón, down right, playing with his ball on a stick. Chipi moves because he doesn't want the writing interrupted.*)

RAMÓN: How're all the gang?

ANASTACIO (*hardly looking at him, with bad humor and abruptly*) :   All right. (*Goes on writing.*)

(*Chipi, jumping off the bench, shakes it. Anastacio curses under his breath.*)

CHIPÍ (*speaking enthusiastically to distract the attention of Ramón*) :   Hello, Ramón! How are things going? (*Approaches him, embraces him, and takes him to one side.*)   How about some maté? Here! Sit down here. (*Practically pushes him onto a bench.*)   Wait, I'll get the cup.

RAMÓN (*looking at Anastacio*) :   What's he doing?

CHIPÍ: Oh, nothing important. Wait a minute. (*Takes down the maté cup. From a pouch, now full, he takes a handful of maté, after first inserting the tube and adding some used maté.*)

RAMÓN: Writing a letter for you?

CHIPÍ: Yes, a short note.

RAMÓN: To Asunción?

CHIPÍ: You're awful inquisitive!

RAMÓN (*imperturbable*) :   To Lola, I suppose.

CHIPÍ (*aggressively*) :   So what?

RAMÓN: Well, there's a pretty and sweet girl here who loves you, and instead, you go looking for Lola.

CHIPÍ: I guess I can pick my own girl.

RAMÓN: It's a pity! (*Thinks a minute.*) I'll bet she's up to no good, way off there in Asunción!

CHIPÍ: Lola? What do you know about Lola?

RAMÓN (*goes on playing with his ball and stick without looking at him*) :   I can guess what she's doing.

ANASTACIO (*completes his writing, and, now that it is not a secret, is impatient*) :   All right, Chipí. Come and read it.

CHIPÍ (*still glaring at Ramón*) :   Let's see what you said.

ANASTACIO (*giving him the paper*) :   You already read the first part. Begin here.

CHIPÍ (*with a gesture*) :   You know I don't know how to read.

RAMÓN (*turning his back and pretending not to pay any attention*) :   Go on and read it to him. I know what it says.

(*Anastacio takes Chipí aside and reads it in a low voice. Chipí nods, but without his previous enthusiasm.*)

ANASTACIO (*in a louder voice*) :   Is it all right?

CHIPÍ (*unenthusiastically*) :   Yes.

ANASTACIO: All right. Let's have your hand. Take this pen. Now, let me move it. Not so stiff.

CHIPÍ (*Smiles, seeing what he is doing.*) :   Is that my name?

ANASTACIO: Yes: Chipí González. (*Starts addressing the envelope.*)

CHIPÍ: That's fine. Now— (*Starts to fold the letter.*)

ANASTACIO: Wait till it's dry. (*Blows it and then presses it against the wall of the house to absorb the ink. Then he folds it and puts it in the envelope. Meantime the dialog goes on.*)

RAMÓN (*suddenly, as if making up his mind*) :   Tell me, Chipí, how are you going to send her the letter?

CHIPÍ: By Mario.

RAMÓN: Mario? That's a good idea. He knows a lot. But talk to him before you send her the letter.

CHIPÍ (*curious*) : What do you mean?

RAMÓN: Nothing! Nothing! Just ask him some questions about Lola. I've nothing more to say.

(*Marta comes in left. She is a graceful girl about seventeen, with dark hair, simply dressed in a flowered garment.*)

MARTA: Good morning!

(*Chipí shows impatience at being interrupted again, when he wants to clear up matters.*)

RAMÓN: Good morning, Marta. (*He approaches and takes her by the arm to one side.*) Why did you come back here again?

MARTA: Papa told me he was coming here.

RAMÓN (*trying to turn her toward him by a hand on her chin*) : That's the only reason?

MARTA (*embarrassed*) : What other reason is there?

RAMÓN (*in her ear*) : I'm wise, and I'm not going to let you play ball by yourself. I'm a fixer, I am!

MARTA (*with downcast eyes, begging him not to carry out his threat*) : But, Ramón—

RAMÓN: That's another matter! But you've got to try hard, Marta.

MARTA: What do you mean?

RAMÓN: You know! (*winking*) You do what I tell you. I'm on your side.

(*All this time, Chipí and Anastacio have been talking. Anastacio seals the envelope and gives it to Chipí. Enter Conche, right, with a jar of water on her head.*)

CONCHE: How's everybody, this morning?

ALL: Good morning, Miss' Conche. (*Some of them speak in Guaraní.*) : Mbaeichapa, na Conche!

CONCHE: I've brought you some cold water.

RAMÓN: I'm sorry I have to leave.

CHIPÍ (*helping her get the jar off her head*):   Don't go yet, Ramón. I want to talk to you. Stay for some more maté.

RAMÓN: No, I've got to go.

CHIPÍ: No, wait. I want to discuss that matter—

RAMÓN: Later, just talk to Mario. (*to Anastacio*) Coming, Anastacio? (*significantly*) Our referee is waiting for us.

CHIPÍ (*visibly displeased*):   Bah! (*Stands as if waiting for something.*)

ANASTACIO: Yes, but we've got to talk to Don Luis first. (*to Marta*) Any idea where your father is?

MARTA: I think he's in the Judge's house.

RAMÓN: We . . . , then, we'll look for him there. (*Winks at Marta.*) 'Bye.

ANASTACIO: Yes, that's an idea. Goodbye, Miss' Conche.

CONCHE: Goodbye.

CHIPÍ: If you see Mario—

ANASTACIO: Yes, I know. (*Exeunt Ramón and Anastacio left.*)

(*Conche goes over and begins grinding corn in a mortar. Chipi sits on a bench, puts his feet on it, and leans his chin on his knees in an attitude of melancholic meditation.*
Marta remains isolated and does not dare go any closer to him. Suddenly she sees the maté cup, left on the table. She pours some water into it from the jar and approaches Chipi. He accepts it and takes a sip, then hands it back without a word. She offers it again, waits a moment and offers it again. Conche continues her rhythmic grinding of corn.)

CHIPÍ: Just me?

MARTA: Yes, I don't want any. (*timidly*) What's the matter, Chipí?

CHIPÍ (*handing back the maté cup*) :   I'm unhappy.

MARTA: Won't you tell me why?

CHIPÍ (*looking at her as if conscious of her for the first time*) :   It's nothing.

MARTA: Nothing?

CHIPÍ (*starting to talk to Marta, then carried away, talks lyrically to himself*) :   At the end of the afternoon, the caretaker puts the football away. The players go home, and I go wandering in the shade of the trees that arch over the path. The stars come out, one here, one there. The smallest ones don't come out yet. One comes out and gets lost again. They're small and far away. I lie on the grass and wait for one to come out, that only I know about. A crazy idea, anyway, hidden the way the stars of the poor are. I'm preparing a nest for it when it arrives. It makes me wait, appearing and disappearing. I lose sight of it. It angers me. It plays with me, but it makes me very happy when I finally find it again.

MARTA: Why are you talking like that, Chipí?

CHIPÍ (*with deep sorrow after a pause*) :   Because this evening, I'm going to be afraid to watch for my star.

MARTA: Poor Chipí! Why don't you come to my house, Chipí?

CHIPÍ: To your house?

MARTA: Yes, I'm sad, too.

CONCHE (*without stopping her grinding*) :   Chipí.

CHIPÍ (*without hearing her*) :   Why are you sad?

MARTA: I'm waiting.

CHIPÍ: Waiting for what?

CONCHE (*still grinding*) :   Chipí!

MARTA: Just waiting.

CHIPÍ (*looking at her tenderly, for a moment*) :   Poor Marta, and you're so pretty. O.K., I'll come to your house. I'll bring my mouth organ.

CONCHE: Chipí!

CHIPÍ (*impatiently*) :   What, Mama?

CONCHE: Don't forget that Pedro is weeding.

CHIPÍ: Yes, Mama. (*to Marta*) I'll bring my mouth organ, and you can sing.

MARTA: Do you like that?

CHIPÍ: I used to do that with Lola.

MARTA (*though annoyed by the reference, gets up and brings the maté cup and offers it to him*) : Here! (*Chipí takes a sip, his mind far away. She shakes her head sadly and makes a pattern in the dirt with her foot. Conche goes on grinding. Enter Luis excitedly from the left, carrying a letter. Anastacio and Mario accompany him, smiling.*)

LUIS: How do you do! Ha ha! Now, the fun begins. There's Chipí, the football star. But where's my old friend?

CONCHE: In the manioc patch.

LUIS: Call him, will you? Right away! It's important!

CONCHE: Heavens! (*She rushes out and can be heard calling.*) Pedro! (*then farther away*) Pedro! (*Meantime the action continues on stage.*)

ANASTACIO (*slapping Chipí's shoulder*) : Well, Chipí, things are starting, old boy!

CHIPÍ: What's happened, Anastá? What's happened?

ANASTACIO: You're going to Asunción.

CHIPÍ: Asunción? How? Do we have a game then? But I don't have a suit to wear.

ANASTACIO: You'll have all the suits you want.

CHIPÍ: Of wool! With regular trousers?

MARIO (*laughing*) : You bet! And with the latest in jackets, and buttons everywhere. And shoes with high heels.

CHIPÍ: Honest? I'm not accustomed to them. But tell me, Anastá, how are we going to Asunción?

(*Enter Pedro right, hurriedly, followed by Conche, out of breath.*)

PEDRO: What's the matter, Luis?

LUIS: Wonderful news! Mario brought a letter from the

National Forward Club. They've sent a contract for
Chipí.

PEDRO: A contract?

LUIS: Yes, the National offers seven hundred thousand
guaraníes for Chipí's release.

PEDRO: Release? What's a release?

LUIS: So he can go to Asunción.

PEDRO: Why? Isn't this land good enough for my head, and
for Conche's and for Chipí?

LUIS: Land, nonsense! What ignorance! What ignorance!
What a lack of public education! A release means that
Chipí is released to the Nationals.

PEDRO: What for?

LUIS: To play football with them, naturally!

PEDRO: And he's going to get seven hundred thousand
guaraníes! How much is that?

ANASTACIO: Seven hundred thousand pesos.

PEDRO: Whee! Seven hundred thousand pesos just to play,
and here we're working all day cutting down weeds just
to eat. I certainly don't understand this world.

ANASTACIO: Aren't you happy about it?

PEDRO (*uncertainly*):   Happy? Seven hundred thousand
pesos to play football. I don't understand yet where the
catch is.

ANASTACIO: Ha, ha! It's evident that Pedro never studied
political economy.

(*Pedro is about to reply, but he is more interested in
what Luis is saying.*)

LUIS: All right, then, Chipí. You've got to get ready to go.

CONCHE: Where is he going?

ANASTACIO: To Asunción—To the Nationals.

CONCHE: I didn't know that. I don't want him to go.

ANASTACIO: But he's going to earn a lot of money, Miss'
Conche. They will pay him a lot of money and give him
a job in the government.

CHIPÍ: But I can't read and write!

MARIO: That doesn't matter. You'll learn everything after you arrive. There were some presidents who had to go to Asunción to learn to write their names.

CHIPÍ: Hurray! Then I can become president, maybe.

MARIO (*maliciously*) : I don't know about president, but you'd be all right as Congressman.

LUIS: Stop that! You sound like a Communist.

MARIO: I was just saying that—

PEDRO: Well, tell me, Luis, when are they going to give us that money?

LUIS: Money? To you? No, sir! That money is for our Club. We're going to finish fencing in the field, so all the spectators will have to pay, and so there won't be any strange cattle messing up the goal posts.

ANASTACIO: That's right, Mr. Commissioner. There'll be no more trouble for the goal keeper when a player kicks a goal. (*Chipí and Mario laugh, perhaps remembering some incident.*)

PEDRO: If Chipí goes away, how will that help him or us?

CONCHE: I don't want my boy to go away.

LUIS: But, Pedro, don't forget the Club has spent a fistful of money on those feet.

PEDRO: If that's true, why do you want to get rid of him?

LUIS: You're crazy, old man. You are obstructing the authority again. If that keeps on, I won't be responsible for your safety.

PEDRO: But that just helps the Club. What about us?

LUIS: What about my double job?

MARTA: When does Chipí have to leave?

ANASTACIO: After the championship match. A commissioner from the Nationals will come to see him play and then fix up everything.

MARTA: Do you want to go, Chipí?

CHIPÍ (*who apparently hadn't asked himself that question,*

tries to decide. All await his reply.) : Yes—I—I guess I do, now.

MARTA: And why now?

CHIPÍ: I don't know, but maybe if I go, something will turn out all right for me.

MARTA: What thing?

CHIPÍ: I don't know. What happens when you suddenly sigh? (*demonstrating*) The wind doesn't oppress you, but the feeling of oppression goes out of you, blown away with the wind of the sigh.

PEDRO (*with his hand on his son's shoulder*) :   I understand, my boy. So it isn't a question of money?

MARTA: Well, father, if he wants to go, who's going to stop him?

LUIS: Come, Anastá. (*to Pedro*) I wanted to bring you the good news myself.

PEDRO: We never know till long afterward whether news is good or bad, Luis.

LUIS: Goodbye for now, old man.

(*Luis, Marta, and Anastacio go off left. Pedro turns to stare at Chipí whose eyes are fixed on the ground. Then he picks up his machete and goes out right to his work, silently, with head bowed. Conche sighs and goes about her tasks.*)

MARIO: Anastá told me you wanted me to take a letter.

CHIPÍ (*as if suddenly rousing*) :   Yes, I did want you to do that for me.

MARIO: All right. Let's have it.

CHIPÍ (*takes out the letter with uncertainty and holds it in front of Mario's eyes, showing him the address*) :   Here it is.

MARIO (*taking it, with a serious expression*) :   Are you still interested in her?

CHIPÍ: Yes.

MARIO (*after a brief hesitation*): Chipí—We come from the same valley. We've played together here. We've had our laughs. We've even fought over kites and tops. We've played on the same teams. Remember the game we used to play—thirty goals, and the loser got a kick in the pants? (*Chipí remembers and laughs nervously, seeing where the other is heading.*) —And that time we had a donkey race, remember?

CHIPÍ: Do you remember the donkey "Doctor?"

MARIO: "Doctor?" Why wouldn't I? It was a fine donkey.

CHIPÍ: Remember when it drank the wine from the barrel in Minetti's store and afterward it took off, after the mare?

MARIO: And a half-crazy mule was the result. (*Both laugh, but Chipí's laugh has a tone of alarmed seriousness.*)

CHIPÍ: Sit down, Mario. Mama, bring us some maté.

CONCHE: All right.

MARIO (*puts his arm on Chipí's shoulder*): Listen, Chipí, we're good friends, practically like brothers, so I must tell you something.

CHIPÍ: What is it, Mario? Let's hear it?

MARIO: Look here, Chipí. You're too good for this woman. (*Gestures to the letter.*)

CHIPÍ: I'd like to know what's wrong with her!

CONCHE: Where did you put the maté cup? Have you seen it, Chipí?

CHIPÍ: No, Mama. I don't know anything about it. Let me alone. (*to Mario*) Tell me what you mean.

CONCHE: Where in heaven's name is that maté cup?

MARIO: Listen, Chipí! You know that women like to ride in up-to-date cars, and go to casinos and night clubs, to wear nylon hose and Cinderella shoes.

CHIPÍ: What are all those things?

MARIO: They're things that cost a lot of money.

CHIPÍ: Are you trying to tell me that Lola lives like that?

MARIO (*nodding his head*): Yes, Chipí. That sort of thing

happens, but there's no point in feeling bad. You can
get dozens of women.

(*Chipí holds his head in his hands, sadly, deeply de-
jected.*)

MARIO: Excuse me, pal, but I had to tell you. It would have
been worse later. With you there alone in Asunción,
who knows what would happen to you? (*Looks at
him.*) Well, I'd better go. I'll be back later. Goodbye,
Miss' Conche! See you later.

(*Chipí slaps him on the shoulders, puts the letter on
the bench, and starts out left.*)

CONCHE: I'm sorry I couldn't find the maté cup.
MARIO: I'll be back this afternoon. Goodbye. (*Exit.*)
CONCHE: Goodbye. (*She brings a tin cup.*) Shall I make
you some maté in this?
CHIPÍ: Don't bother, Mama!
CONCHE: Don't you want it now?
CHIPÍ: No, not now.
CONCHE: My boy, aren't you glad you're going?
CHIPÍ: I don't know.
CONCHE: Don't you want to go? I didn't want you to go,
but when I saw you wanted to, I made up my mind.
You'll have lots of things there that you can't have here.
(*Looks tenderly at him, but Chipí does not reply.*)
Cheer up, boy! You see I want you to go, too. All I ask
is that you don't forget your old mother.
CHIPÍ (*distractedly*):   No, Mama.
CONCHE: Our valley is poor. People from other places don't
come here, and those from here go away—one to work,
one after a woman, one to study, one on account of a
revolution. Always for something. They don't want to
go, maybe, but what is there to keep them here? Here
they have nothing. Not their land, or their work, not
even plants or cattle to look after. What's to hold them?

Nothing except their heart. So they leave their heart behind and go away. (*She puts a hand on his hand.*) Poor Chipí, poor boy! (*She wipes away a tear, secretly.*) I promise not to say anything more to you. I won't cry, so you won't be so unhappy to leave the valley.

CHIPÍ (*getting up impetuously*): Mama, please! I can't stand it. (*He starts off hurriedly, then hesitates, and comes back. He picks up the letter and tears it into little bits. He throws them down angrily and rushes off, left.*)

CONCHE (*upset*): What's the matter with him? The poor boy! And I was saying silly things to him. (*She turns slowly as if to enter the house—the lights on the stage dim out, as she exits.*)

(*The light on the cloud comes up. Saul is trying to get the tube out of the maté cup that disappeared. Mom looks on with a superior smile. He asks by gestures for the maté cup and Saul gives it to him with a gesture of helplessness. Mom smiles devilishly.*)

MOM: And you're an angel! (*He pulls out the tube, cleans it off, replaces it carefully. Takes a sip, and passes it back to Saul.*)

SAUL (*smiles, a little disgustedly*): You're a devil!

MOM: Your vision of the future seems to be working out.

SAUL (*shrugging his shoulders*): It was all documented.

MOM: A fine way of registering acts.

SAUL: But too simple. A human act is a visible spark from a collision between the past and the future.

MOM: Don't complicate it too much.

SAUL: I've still left out the mysterious part.

MOM (*ironically*): What's that?

SAUL: You remember that harmony reigned in Eden. When that place was abandoned, somebody forgot a harp hanging in the branches of a laurel tree. The breeze still weaves its caprices through it, and in mo-

ments when man gives way to solitude, he thinks he can
find in the depths of himself an unknown melody.

MOM: Then what happens?

SAUL: He remains a prisoner of his enchantment. He has
heard a strange something that assures him that the
infinite passes through him. And ever after, he'll do all
sorts of things to hear again the far-off harmony that he
thinks he recognizes. Perhaps—

MOM: You complicate things too much. If any human act
could be that diabolically—I mean angelically—complicated, I don't know how our technical experts could
ever figure out whether the person acting like that will
be condemned or not.

SAUL: That infernal invention still amazes me.

MOM: Maybe. (*suddenly conscious of the scene below*) But
look! There's something new.

(*The light on the cloud is extinguished and the lower
stage is lighted. Enter Chipí completely drunk, held up
by Marta.*)

CHIPÍ: Hurray for the big game! Hurray for the Night
Club! (*He staggers and almost falls, pulling Marta
along.*)

MARTA: Yes, Chipí. Hurray! Come over here, to the cot.

CHIPÍ: Why should I lie down? Me? I'm not drunk. Not
completely drunk.

MARTA: Of course not. You're not drunk, but come and sit
down here and you'll feel better. (*Tries to get him to
the cot.*)

CHIPÍ: No—I don't want to—hic—sit there! Hurray for
night clubs! I'm going to Asunción to play for the
Nationals, because I'm a star, a great star. And I'll see
her. They say she goes in for nylon stockings and trans-
parent plastic shoes and casinos and night clubs. I'm
going to see her.

MARTA: Yes, Chipí—Of course you're going to see her—Sit
here. (*Leads him to a bench.*) Wait here. I'll get some
water to wash your face. (*She goes for a jug of water
and Chipí lies back on the bench, but when he tries to
pull up his feet, he and the bench tip over.*) What
happened to you? (*She hurries back to help him.*)

CHIPÍ: Confound it, the bench upset. (*Tries to get up, but
gets tangled up and falls again.*)

MARTA: I told you to lie on the cot, but you *would* do
things your way! (*She tries to help him up, but Chipí is
beyond help.*)

CHIPÍ: It was because the bench was no good. They ought
to throw it away! (*He strikes out at it, then falls to the
ground.*)

MARTA: No, Chipí! (*She shakes her head, sits on the
ground beside him and rests his head on her lap. He is
muttering, unconscious. Finally he falls asleep. She
smooths back his hair and weeps silently.*)

CURTAIN

ACT 3
Scene 1—Afternoon

*When the curtain rises, shouts and distant cheers are
heard from an unseen crowd watching a football game.
Pedro walks back and forth, frantic. Conche is also worried.*

PEDRO: We're losing. Two to nothing. First they were all
cheering for Chipí, then after the goal, the other side
shouted.

CONCHE: What was Chipí doing?

PEDRO: Running around the field like an orphan calf. Luis
grabbed me and said: "Is that the way your Chipí
plays?" I told him: "A game is a game, Luis." And he
said: "Yes, that's what he's supposed to be playing."

And they all began yelling "That's the stuff!" and that old fool pushed against me.

CONCHE: Heavens. I can't believe it.

PEDRO: Yes, indeed. "No, sir!" I told him. "Respect the Commissioner," he shouted and shoved me again. "Then he'll give me permission, too," I told him, and I drew back and swung my machete.

CONCHE: Heavens! That's why you ran away?

PEDRO: The Commissioner came after me, my old friend, and he shouted: "Let that guy go, you fool. I'm sure you're drunk, just like your son!" I dropped my machete and came away. Me drunk? When has anybody ever seen me drunk?

CONCHE: What a hateful person! Sit down, Pedro, and take it easy.

PEDRO: Tell me something, Conche, did you ever see Chipí drinking before?

CONCHE: Don't mention it to me! But recently, he's been drinking like crazy.

PEDRO: Where did he ever get started?

CONCHE: I don't know what's got into him. The first time I ever saw him that way was when he was lying on the ground with Marta holding his head.

PEDRO: Yes, I know. It was awful. I smelled it for days.

CONCHE: Didn't you say anything to him?

PEDRO: I talked, but (*Shrugs.*) where can you find words to convince a boy? You've got to be wiser than a witch doctor.

CONCHE: I tried to say something, too, but he answered me back. The only one able to do anything with him is Marta, poor girl. Do you think she likes him?

PEDRO: Likes him? (*Ponders.*) Well, not any longer. And it wouldn't do any good if she did.

CONCHE: Why not?

PEDRO: On account of what's happened. I'm sure Chipí has nothing to do with her father any more, and we don't,

either. They aren't going to let her come anywhere near
here.

CONCHE: Because he played so badly, today?

PEDRO: Of course! If he's no longer a star, that ends it. The
old man won't let her have anything to do with a
ruined gaucho. Now her father is a big merchant. (*as if
reading a sign*) Police Station, grocery, and hardware
store. "Prosperity of the Valley!" Now when he talks
about us, he calls us "those people." (*a burst of yelling,
with the word "goal" distinguishable*)

CONCHE: Did you hear that, Pedro? Chipí has made a goal.

PEDRO (*excited*) :   Confound it, how I'd like to go back and
see.

CONCHE: Shall I go?

PEDRO: Yes, go ahead. (*She starts but he stops her.*) What
am I going to do here alone? Wait! I told Ramón to
bring me word if anything happened. (*more yells and
sounds of shouts*)

CONCHE: Maybe the goal was against us! Virgin of Caacupé,
help me!

PEDRO (*starts running out left*) :   I'm going to see. (*Stops.
Searches in his belt for a weapon.*) Look! Here comes
Ramón. (*shouting*) Ramón, what's going on? What's
happening?

RAMÓN (*inside, shouting*) :   Another score against us.

PEDRO: Against us?

RAMÓN (*coming in left*) :   Yes, against us. The crowd
rushed onto the field and the referee allowed an onside
kick.

PEDRO: What?

RAMÓN: Yes, the referee, that bandit, let them take the ball
for a free kick on the field, but the Commissioner came
riding out, and they tangled!

PEDRO: Did you ever hear of anything so unfair!

RAMÓN: It sure was! But the Commissioner jumped on the
referee and shouted: "Offside? You're crazy!"

CONCHE: Old Luis is a fighter, got to give him credit for that.

PEDRO: And what did that miserable referee say?

RAMÓN: "Very well, not offside, then," he said, but Cachi, the captain of the Presidents team, pulled up his jersey like this, and yanked out a knife. God help me!

CONCHE: Holy Mary!

PEDRO: Then what? Then what? What happened? Why did I ever leave?

RAMÓN: The Commissioner shouted: "Stop it. Don't you move, you so and so! I'm going to turn you over to the authorities." He took out his revolver, and shot over the captain's head and rode over him on his horse. Cachi fell, but all the Presidents ran in with knives, machetes, and revolvers, and the spectators came in, too, from all sides.

PEDRO: What about the referee?

RAMÓN: He started running, but one of the Presidents chased him and cut at him. Lord help me! But he was lucky. (*Indicates a cut across his face.*) All he lost was part of his ear, but as pay for what he did, that wasn't bad. Goodbye, referee! He took off for the other side of the mountain.

CONCHE: What about Chipí? Haven't you seen him?

RAMÓN (*disconcerted*): No, I haven't seen him, but when I left nobody had been killed yet.

CONCHE: You didn't see him?

RAMÓN: No, but he must still be fighting.

CONCHE: Pedro, go and look for him.

PEDRO: Right away! (*He runs into the house and gets a shotgun.*) Coming, Ramón?

RAMÓN: I'm right behind you. Yippee! (*Both rush out, left.*)

CONCHE: Where could Chipí be? Virgin of Caacupé, protect me! I promise to go on foot to church, with a jug of water on my head, to give a drink to every pilgrim who is thirsty. Don't let anything happen to him, Blessed Virgin! (*Enter Chipí, left, running, with his football uniform torn.*)

CONCHE: Heavens, Chipí, my boy! What happened? What have they done to you?

CHIPÍ (*gasping and looking for a place to hide*) : Where's the shotgun? (*Starts inside to look for it.*)

CONCHE: What happened? Pedro took the gun to go looking for you. I'll call him! (*Starts out.*) Pedro! Pedro!

CHIPÍ (*worried*) : No, Mama. Let him go! Keep quiet. I've got to hide. (*Seizes a pair of trousers and a shirt, and puts them on hastily, while the conversation continues.*)

CONCHE: Why? What did you do?

CHIPÍ: Nothing, Mama, but they all think I sold them out. I've got to hide. (*He looks about. Conche points out a basket beside the porch.*)

CONCHE: Here, my boy. I'll put some clothes over you. (*Chipi hides and she throws some clothes on top. Enter a Fan left, with a machete in his hand.*)

FAN I: That bandit must be somewhere around here.

(*Enter three more Fans, dragging Pedro along. They have taken away his gun. They carry knives, guns, and clubs.*)

FAN II: Search his room. He probably hid there under the bed. (*Two run into the house.*)

PEDRO: I told them he wasn't here, and I also told them Chipí would never sell them out.

FAN I: Shut up, you mangy old man! Tell us where that scoundrel went.

PEDRO: You're mangy yourself. You swayback horse! To come and tear up my house.

FAN II: We'll rip you up, too, if we don't find that traitor.

CONCHE: Well, rip it up then if you can, you good-for-nothing.

FAN II: What good does it do to talk to these two? They've

already hidden the money. Let's go look for the two-timer.

FAN I: Yes, we'll leave these two. What we want is that traitor.

FAN II: You take a look around the judge's yard, and we'll meet you in front of the Commissioner's store.

FAN I: Well, hurry up. We mustn't let him get to the mountain. He knows all the hiding places there. (*Fans I and III start out, right.*)

PEDRO: Are you going to steal my gun, too?

FAN II: Steal? Steal? We're not like you. Leave that filthy thing. (*Fan III, who carried the shotgun, throws it scornfully to the ground and goes out.*)

FAN II: We'll go this way. (*He and Fan IV start out left, but meet Luis and Anastacio, who are coming in. Luis is angry. Anastacio carries the trophy cup.*)

LUIS: Where's that bandit?

FAN I: We've been looking for him, too, Mr. Commissioner.

LUIS: Didn't he come here?

FAN II: We've looked everywhere. There's a patrol out there and we were going the other direction.

LUIS: He mustn't be allowed to get away with it. He's got to receive his punishment as an example. He's trying to get away with the cash.

ANASTACIO: We must get his confession. We can't lose the cup that way. (*Holds it up.*)

LUIS: Lose the cup? I should say not! That's why we're here, to make the principles of authority respected. Take that cup to the jeweler right away and get the name of our glorious club engraved on it.

ANASTACIO: Are we going to get it engraved before we present our protest?

LUIS: Of course! Have the name of the club engraved there, at the expense of the police department. Why am I commissioner if I can't have done whatever I want?

FAN II: Oh, Commissioner, it's sportsmen like you who bring fame to our glorious clubs! (*to Fan IV*) Let's go and look for that good-for-nothing! (*Exeunt left.*)

ANASTACIO: Well, Mr. Commissioner, all we need now is to find the referee who ran off to the mountain.

LUIS: Didn't the Presidents escape to the mountains, too?

ANASTACIO: Like a flash! They didn't even wait to get their clothes.

LUIS: Well, the insects drive the cattle out of the mountain, maybe the Presidents will drive out the referee, too.

ANASTACIO: But if they find him— (*Gestures a cut throat.*)

LUIS: Good Lord! And we need him, don't we?

ANASTACIO: You know, Mr. Commissioner, that the referee was always on our side. Later! (*significantly*) With the influence you hold over him, well, confound it, if you ask him on the right terms, he'll say that the Presidents walked off the field, and that he saw the money being turned over to our player.

CONCHE: Heavens! What a lie! If the referee says that, I'll look after that mangy dog myself.

PEDRO: Hush, Conche, you're old and toothless. You'll have to keep quiet.

LUIS: You're right. Toothless people have to learn to swallow without biting. And to respect authority. (*to Anastacio*) Let's settle the matter.

ANASTACIO: Shall we go to the Judge's house and lodge the protest?

LUIS: That's a good idea, and I'll send some policemen to bring back the referee, to make sure. (*to Pedro, angrily*) And you! We'll settle with you later, as an example. (*Exit with Anastacio, left. About the middle of the last scene Marta has appeared in the wings, down right. As soon as the others leave, Pedro picks up his gun, looks to the loading and goes into the house. Enter Marta, wiping away her tears. When Conche sees her, she asks in gestures if anybody is around.*)

CONCHE: They've all gone.

MARTA (*throwing herself into Conche's arms*) :   Oh, Miss'
Conche, it isn't true what they're saying, is it?

CONCHE: Of course not!

MARTA: Chipí wouldn't lose the game on purpose! He
wouldn't go back on his friends, especially for money.

CONCHE: God forbid! He'd never do that.

MARTA: It's all the fault of that woman! She's to blame,
Miss' Conche.

CONCHE (*trying to lead her from Chipí's hiding place so he
won't hear*) :   What woman, Marta? Tell me.

MARTA: That Lola. She did something to him, and ever
since, he's been crazy, getting drunk without paying
attention to anything or anybody.

CONCHE (*Tries to pull her farther away, but Chipí sticks his
head out to listen.*) :   What did she do? How did you
know about it?

MARTA (*angrily*) :   Why shouldn't I know? When he gets
drunk, all he does is repeat her name. But Chipí is
good, Miss' Conche. I know he's good. If I could only
do something to help him get rid of his nightmare.

CONCHE (*now trying to drag her toward the basket*) :   You
love him, don't you, Marta?

MARTA (*embracing her and weeping*) :   Yes, Miss' Conche.

CHIPÍ (*coming noisily out of his hiding place*) :   Marta!
Dear little Marta!

CONCHE (*alarmed*) :   Why didn't you stay there?

MARTA: Heavens! You here? (*She turns away embarrassed.*)

CHIPÍ: Forgive me, Marta!

MARTA: Get back and hide, quick! They'll be back here any
minute.

PEDRO (*coming out of the house hurriedly*) :   What's going
on? Who's coming? (*He carries his gun. He sees
Chipí.*) Where did you come from? Did they hurt
you, my boy?

CHIPÍ: No, Papa, I'm all right. I hid.

PEDRO: And now what are you going to do?

CHIPÍ: I'm going to the mountain, and then later, I'm going—

PEDRO: You don't need to go very far. You know things will be fixed.

CHIPÍ: No, Papa. I'm leaving.

PEDRO: You mean you're going for good?

CHIPÍ: Yes.

PEDRO (*nodding his head*):   Yes, my son. I knew that you were getting an urge to leave. The same thing happened to me. I don't know what it is. It's like a dream that tells you every night that you're not here, that you're somewhere else. When you wake up, you don't remember the dream, but you start looking in every direction, and suddenly you realize that the sky doesn't end above the mountain, and the road looks at you like a beautiful woman with her face veiled. Then if you don't have deep roots, you go away. For us Paraguayans who hardly have roots to start with, there's always a commissioner who keeps cutting at the roots we do have. (*With his head bent, he is lost in his thoughts, but suddenly he looks at the gun in his hand.*) I'm going to put a load in this! (*Hurries into the house to hide his emotions. Chipí is silent, not knowing how to reply. The others say nothing.*)

CONCHE (*in a timid voice*):   And you're going, like this?

CHIPÍ: This is my chance. Everything has gone wrong. Mama, tie my things in my poncho, will you?

CONCHE (*after a gesture of protest, starts toward the house*):   But why can't we wait—?

CHIPÍ: Before I leave, Marta, I wanted to tell you something.

MARTA: What?

CHIPÍ: That I'll come back and I won't forget that you are my blessing. That when I fell, you helped me up. And now that it's all over, I suspect that sometimes I fell just to get your help.

MARTA *(coming closer)*: What do you mean, Chipí?

CHIPÍ: Now that I'm leaving, I look at you and it seems— The Commissioner hasn't cut the root that links me to you. I think it was too deep underneath.

MARTA: Why do you tell me this now?

CHIPÍ: Because I'm coming back. I'm leaving so I can forget the fellow who died today running after a football. I'm leaving, so when I come back and tell you all I have to tell you, you'll trust me.

CONCHE *(appearing with a poncho tied so it can be carried, bandit style. She has put food into two bags)*: You're in such a hurry!

MARTA: No, Chipí, you don't need to come back for that. Chipí, take me with you, now.

CHIPÍ: What? What did you say?

MARTA: Take me with you!

CHIPÍ: But I'm going into the mountains and I don't know where.

MARTA: All right. Then I'm coming along.

CHIPÍ: Do you know what you're saying, Marta?

MARTA: Of course. You made me cry too much last time you went away to let you do it again. Listen, I'll go and get some horses from papa. The mare is mine. He gave it to me. I'll bring them to the gate of the meadow. Meet me there.

CHIPÍ *(takes her by the shoulders and looks into her face)*: Do you have courage enough to face the mountain and all that we don't know about, unprotected, with only your hands, and to give up everything?

MARTA: You know I have.

CHIPÍ: Then I know why the commissioner couldn't cut my roots, because to me you are this valley. This land of mine that can withstand everything, give everything, wait forever, will always be in my heart. Come, sweetheart! (*They embrace.*)

CONCHE (*with the packages, looks at them astonished, but makes no comment*) : I think you have everything.

CHIPÍ: Let me have it, Mama. (*He hangs it from his shoulder.*)

PEDRO (*coming out of the house with the gun and cartridges tied in a rag*) : Here, my boy, and here's the powder and shot.

CHIPÍ: Thank you, Papa! Mama, Marta and I are leaving together. We want your blessing.

CONCHE: Heavens, what are you going to do?

PEDRO: Think it over, my boy. In times like this a woman is a burden.

CHIPÍ: She won't be a burden if it's a pleasure to take her. We've got to find where that sky goes, that you talked about, the one that doesn't end above the mountain.

PEDRO: Very well, my boy. Around here, that's the way we all start. So God bless you both. (*Blesses them.*)

CONCHE: But don't you think you'd better wait till night?

CHIPÍ: No, Mama. It's getting dark already. And besides we have two horses. (*He embraces her.*)

CONCHE: Goodbye, my son. May God bless you, and you, too, Marta. (*She embraces her and blesses her.*)

CHIPÍ (*Hands the bundle to Marta and he takes the gun.*) : No one will catch us. And we'll be back!

MARTA: Goodbye till then. (*She follows Chipi out right.*)

PEDRO and CONCHE: Goodbye, goodbye, children!

(*They continue staring after them. Conche wipes her eyes with the corner of her skirt.*)

PEDRO: They've gone.

(*Conche nods her head, resigned, and keeps on crying.*)

PEDRO (*putting an arm over her shoulder*) : Don't cry, Conche. That's the way it has to be.

(*Conche nods again.*)

PEDRO: So we're alone again. (*She nods.*) Well, that's the way things are. Come here. Sit here, my poor old lady. (*He takes her to a bench where she sits down.*) Don't you want me to make you some maté?

CONCHE (*shakes her head*) :   You don't think they'll catch him?

PEDRO: Of course not! He knows all the mountain paths.

CONCHE: Why wouldn't he wait till night?

PEDRO: It's already dark. (*He lights the lantern.*)

CONCHE (*still wiping her eyes*) :   It's the fault of that other woman.

PEDRO: It's the fault of something. (*He hangs up the lantern and sits near her.*) We Paraguayans are like those clumps of water lilies. The river flows under us and we say: "Goodbye, we're leaving." The shadow of a cloud passes over the water. We think it's a boat. We're hardly settled. And up comes another strong wind and off we go.

CONCHE: Where?

PEDRO: Off to look for our hope. The valley offers little hope. We men are flesh and blood, but we have our illusion. Our flesh takes us various places, to the fields, to the yerba maté plantations, but we look for the most beautiful, the safest place to plant our illusions. (*with emphasis*) That's why nobody plants illusions in other people's fields. That's why roots don't grow. Here we're only shallow-rooted, and when the time comes, it doesn't take much to make us leave.

CONCHE: But why does all this happen?

PEDRO: Because they won't let us put down roots. Because we are just shallow-rooted. Ha ha! In life we always need a roof over us; but we aren't afraid to leave it.

There's nothing to keep us tied to a place except roots
we put down, our own illusions. Nothing else will hold
us.

CONCHE: Why didn't you tell all this to Chipí before he
went away?

PEDRO: Because he wouldn't understand. He thinks he's
leaving just because of the football, and the Commissioner, and that woman. Of course he is leaving on
account of them. But behind it all, are his illusions. It's
like a witch glow in the dark night of that desert. It
dazzles, attracts, and lures, until you leave your path
and go toward the mysterious glow.

CONCHE: I didn't want him to grow up.

*(Enter Luis and Anastacio, left. Luis carries a rolled
official document.)*

LUIS: Now that we have this, ha, ha—the Presidents aren't
going to win the match. We'll see to that! Ha ha!

ANASTACIO: Our protest sounds fine! There's nothing the
other team can do.

LUIS: Our judge is really formidable. How quickly he
understood everything. He could give only one answer.

ANASTACIO: That's the way a good functionary is.

LUIS: You're right. There's no denying it. But how could
anything be wrong with it when a Public Accountant,
an honorable judge, and a distinguished commissioner
drew it up!

ANASTACIO: There can't be any error!

LUIS: The Presidents couldn't get away with it even with
an army. What an example it sets.

ANASTACIO: All we need now is Pedro's signature.

LUIS: That's right. That's why we came. The judge said it
would be a good idea for him to sign. Then nobody
could say anything. *(to Pedro)* Look, Pedro, I want a
word with you.

PEDRO: Are you speaking to me, Mr. Commissioner?

LUIS: Of course. Is there any other Pedro around here?

PEDRO: Oh! I thought you had forgotten all about me.

LUIS: How could I forget you? Everything is all right again, so how about a little help? Will you just make your thumb mark here. (*Points to the paper.*)

CONCHE: Pedro, be careful about what they want you to do.

LUIS: What do we want him to do? We're not asking him for money. All we ask is cooperation with the authorities and just with one finger. Surely he'd lend one finger to help the work of the government.

(*Enter Fan I from the right hurriedly.*)

FAN I: Mr. Commissioner! Mr. Commissioner!

LUIS: What is it? What's the matter?

FAN I: It's Chipí, on your spotted horse! He's riding like a bullet toward the mountain. All you can see is dust.

LUIS: Damn him! You say that miserable rascal is riding Old Spot?

FAN I: And your daughter Marta is riding beside him on your mare.

LUIS: Damn and damn! That's what I call horse stealing. (*He grabs Pedro by the shirt.*) What have you to say, you—? You—?

PEDRO: Me? Why—

LUIS (*shouting*):   Tell me! What's happening, señor?

PEDRO: Me? I—I don't know, Mr. Commissioner.

LUIS: What do you mean, you don't know? Isn't your worthless son stealing my daughter and two horses? (*Releases him and turns to the Fan.*) Go back to the Police Station and order a squad to ride after him.

FAN I: All the fans are out looking for the referee, Sir. And there's only one fan there, with an old Bolivian rifle that doesn't have a trigger.

LUIS: Something must be done! What can we do, Anastacio?

ANASTACIO (*perplexed*): I don't know. Why not consult the judge?

LUIS (*delighted*): That's the idea! (*to Fan I*) Go and call the judge. Tell him to bring all his books.

FAN I: All his books?

LUIS: Yes, every one, and ink and a lot of pens and official paper.

FAN I: Doggone! That's the end of Chipí González. (*Rushes out right. Meantime Luis paces up and down.*)

LUIS (*angrily*): The nerve of him! And I used to admire him! What's the authority coming to? But just let him wait. I'll catch that mangy rascal. He won't get away with it!

RAMÓN (*entering left*): Good evening! (*The only one giving him a clear answer is Anastacio. Pedro and Conche hardly raise their voices, knowing they are in trouble, without any of the constitutional guarantees of rights. Luis is too angry to listen.*)

ANASTACIO: Good evening!

RAMÓN: Mr. Commissioner, the representative of the Nationals wants a few words with you before he takes his bus. (*Luis is too furious to reply.*)

RAMÓN (*going on, somewhat disconcerted*): He wanted to say goodbye to you before leaving. (*still no answer*) He says the matter of player transfer no longer interests him because he saw that lousy game. (*Anastacio makes signs to him to stop; but Ramón does not see them and goes on.*) Maybe in some of the games Chipí makes a goal from mid-field, but (*mocking him*) "No, thank you, Mr. Commissioner, Mr. Storekeeper." Once he made a goal with his head. Once with his feet, and once with the referee. Miracles don't happen every day. I told him he'd seen Chipí on a bad day. "You ought to see his change of pace and the kick he can let go," I told him.

(*He goes nearer to Luis in spite of Anastacio's signs.*) Isn't that true, Mr. Commissioner?

LUIS (*unable to control himself, explodes*): Leave me alone! I never want to hear his name again. Here's your protest! (*He tears it up and throws it at Anastacio.*) Do what you like with it. If you want to sell Chipí, you'll first have to track him down.

RAMÓN (*disconcerted*): Very well, Mr. Commissioner. If you say so— (*He does not understand what is going on.*)

LUIS: All right. I want no more discussion. Get out of here, all of you. (*to Anastacio*) I mean you, too.

ANASTACIO (*frightened*): Very well, Mr. Commissioner. We're leaving.

(*He and Ramón exeunt rapidly, left, just as the judge enters. He is a lean man with a cynical face. He wears a much-worn tropical suit, with mends and stains, a stained necktie, raveled shirt, glasses, and old felt hat. He comes in more hurriedly than his strength permits. He carries several books and an ink bottle hanging from a string.*)

JUDGE (*to all*): Good evening. (*Without more ceremony he approaches Luis.*) Mr. Commissioner! (*gasping*) I came as fast as I could to offer my services, Mr. Commissioner!

LUIS: Yes, Your Honor, we've got a serious case.

JUDGE (*his expression grows solemn*: To apply the law, and if necessary, a wise interpretation of the law.

LUIS: Chipí González ran away with my daughter and stole two horses from me.

JUDGE (*professionally*): Kidnapping and grand larceny!

LUIS: What shall we do, Your Honor?

JUDGE: According to the law, we can bring charges.

LUIS: Charges? So we can go after him and arrest him? I

can go after him without bringing charges if I thought I could catch him, but since I can't lay hands on him, I want to get back at him some other way.

JUDGE: Ah, well then, we'll have to proceed according to a judicial interpretation of the law.

LUIS: I want to make sure that rascal doesn't think he outsmarted me!

JUDGE: That's quite simple. If Chipí González marries your daughter, then legally he didn't kidnap her, and he didn't steal any horses from you because according to the penal code, children cannot rob their parents.

LUIS: Magnificent! Then he's the one that's fooled! He steals my horses, but he can't steal my horses. He steals my daughter, but he can't steal my daughter! So he hasn't outsmarted me after all!

JUDGE: Exactly.

LUIS: Can we marry them, ourselves?

JUDGE (*showing the books*): Here are my tools. Shall we get at it at once?

LUIS: Right away!

(*The Judge looks for a place to write on one of the benches. He sits on a chair, selects a book and opens it.*)

JUDGE: Light! (*Fan I brings the lantern closer. The Judge gives him the ink bottle to hold.*) What's Chipí's name?

LUIS: Cipriano González, alias Chipí.

JUDGE (*writing*): Paraguayan, bachelor, a minor. (*Looking over his glasses at Luis.*) His father, Pedro González, also agrees to the marriage?

LUIS: Of course! Of course!

JUDGE: Very well. If he doesn't, I can appoint a temporary guardian. It's the same thing. (*Writes.*) Marta Benítez, Paraguayan, unmarried, and so forth—We can fill that in afterward.

CONCHE: What are you doing?

LUIS: You'll find out later.

JUDGE (*gets up with his book and looks for a pamphlet*) : Let's get on with the ceremony. The contracting parties stand here before me. (*Luis takes his place there.*) Now, I'll hear the necessary declarations. Do you, Cipriano González, take for spouse and wife, Marta Benítez?

LUIS: Yes, I do!

JUDGE: Do you, Marta Benítez, accept as spouse and husband, Cipriano González?

LUIS: Yes, I accept him.

JUDGE: Then in conformity with the powers that the law grants me, I declare you man and wife. The law requires that after the official ceremony I must read articles 50, 51, and 53 of the Civil Matrimonial Code, but since they cannot plead ignorance of the law, interpreting it judicially, I shall omit that part. (*He clears his throat.*) And now, gentlemen, let us sign the records. For Chipí González and Marta Benítez at their request and because they cannot write, I shall append their signatures. Now, Pedro González, will you sign here as evidence of your consent. (*Indicates the place in the book.*)

PEDRO: What have I got to sign?

JUDGE: You heard what was going on. The marriage papers for your son Chipí and Marta Benítez.

PEDRO: Do you mean they're married?

LUIS: Weren't you a witness? What ignorance! What a need for public instruction!

CONCHE: So Chipí is married, then?

LUIS: Of course he's married.

CONCHE: God forgive us! Not a note of music at the wedding!

LUIS: Go ahead! Sign!

PEDRO: I don't know how to write.

JUDGE (*Takes a stamping pad out of his pocket*) : Then as

a verification, your finger print. (*He inks Pedro's thumb.*)

CONCHE: Pedro, what are you doing?

(*Pedro shrugs his shoulders and lets them apply his thumb to the paper.*)

JUDGE: Good. Now, for the girl, you, Mr. Commissioner. (*Hands Luis the pen. Luis extends his thumb.*) Don't you know how to write, Mr. Commissioner?

LUIS: Oh, must I sign? (*uneasily*) All right, then. But later in my office. I'm feeling too indisposed to sign now.

JUDGE: Very well. I'll take care of the rest of the witnesses. (*Closes the book.*) Gentlemen, the ceremony is over. There is nothing left for me except to congratulate the contracting parties and wish them many years of happiness together. (*Shakes hands with Luis.*)

LUIS: Thank you, Your Honor. Collaboration and understanding between the authorities is what makes this country progress.

JUDGE: Of course! Now tell me. My fees are to be paid by the family of the groom?

LUIS: No, Your Honor. We'll settle that. The first good prisoner we arrest will settle for everything.

JUDGE: All right. I understand.

LUIS (*shaking hands with Pedro*):   Well, Pedro, to show you that things can be arranged between friends, the suit between you and me is also settled.

PEDRO (*shaking hands somewhat perplexed*):   Yes, that's right. That's right.

LUIS: And Conche, since we're now one family, congratulations! (*He embraces her.*)

CONCHE: Thanks. Can Chipí come back now?

LUIS: Of course. He's my son now. He has full protection. And I want to show him he can't outsmart me. As for the game, if anybody says he sold out his team, he'll have to settle with me.

CONCHE: How lucky! We just happened to hear where he went, so we can send for him.

LUIS: Good. Ha ha! It will be all arranged as a family affair. Won't you come to my house to celebrate? You're all welcome, Judge and all.

PEDRO: Thank you. We'll come later. I've got to put on my other clothes.

LUIS: We'll be expecting you. Come soon!

PEDRO and CONCHE: Very soon! (*Exeunt Luis, Judge and Fan I, left. Pedro and Conche stand looking at each other, still not entirely understanding.*)

CONCHE: What good luck! Chipí is coming back again!

PEDRO: We don't know. It was his idea to go away.

CONCHE: But now he's got guarantees.

PEDRO: Yes, but who knows whether he'll want to come? But don't worry, Conche. It'll turn out. He's happy. He still thinks life is beautiful. And therefore, life is beautiful for him. (*He pats her lovingly.*) Go on, old lady, will you? Bring me my clean shirt.

(*Conche goes into the house. Pedro begins to take off the shirt he is wearing, but in the process he starts thinking and slows up. Suddenly he reveals surprise and begins laughing. Conche comes out with the shirt and hands it to him. He puts it on, still laughing.*)

CONCHE: What are you laughing about? Tell me!

PEDRO: You didn't remember, did you? That marriage ceremony isn't any good. (*He puts his hand on her shoulder.*) Have you forgotten that Chipí isn't Chipí González? When I found you in the deserted regions of the Upper Paraná, you'd already borne the boy? He's the son of that man Torres who got lost in the jungles and died.

CONCHE: Yes, he's the son of Torres.

PEDRO: Then he isn't Chipí González. He's Chipí Torres.

Don't you remember? All those words they wrote in the big book aren't worth anything.

CONCHE: Oh, my God! What shall we do?

PEDRO (*taking the lantern and starting out, left*) :   Nothing. Never let them know. Let's go and celebrate the marriage of a nobody who's called Chipí González. Ha ha ha! (*Exeunt.*)

(*Enter Mom left, leafing through a huge volume. Saul follows, interested.*)

MOM: Torres—Torres Ciriaco? (*He shakes his head.*) I've looked in all the records, and I can't find his name, not even in the list of doubtful ones. (*Shuts his book.*) No, he's not here. Cipriano Torres, alias Chipí González doesn't appear! And I was so sure he would go to Hell.

SAUL: So he's not condemned?

MOM: I don't know what will happen to him.

SAUL: Neither do I. It's disconcerting, isn't it? A demon, an angel, a powerful commissioner, a crafty judge, a football team, and a woman, all wanted to get their hands on Chipí, in one form or other, and he escapes us all.

MOM: We hadn't foreseen all the possibilities. He escaped through some loophole that we didn't watch.

SAUL: We can never stop up all the loopholes.

MOM: Why not?

SAUL: Because deep in every human being, God put a crazy auger that can drill out a loophole anywhere.

MOM: An auger? What sort of auger?

SAUL: What it is, nobody knows exactly, but it's called "love of liberty."

CURTAIN

The Man of the Century

A COMEDY IN THREE ACTS

CHARACTERS
Estela González, *the mother*
Daniel, *her husband*
George, *their son*
Marisol, *their daughter*
Cecilio Paniagua

ACT 1

Action in present-day Santiago de Chile.

The setting: the living room of the elegant González third-floor apartment. Furniture and drapes are expensive, clearly showing the prosperity of Daniel González, the father. A slight air of nouveau-riche emanates from the room. Nevertheless, the color scheme is in good taste. The glass door at the rear leads into the entrance hall. When it is open, one sees the hall from which one door opens into adjoining rooms and another is the main entrance to the apartment. On both sides of the glass door stand statues of Venetian slaves. (Left and right are from the audience's point of view.) *To the left, in one corner of the room is a beautiful marble fireplace above which hangs a showy oil painting of Estela in the role of Shakespeare's Juliet. Farther downstage, a window opening onto the balcony, but now heavy brocaded curtains are drawn. A double door, right, leads to the dining room.*

On the walls, a few Chinese prints so simple that they contrast with the exuberance of the other room decorations, especially with the portrait of the mistress of the house. In front of the fireplace, a comfortable sofa upholstered in yellow brocade and flanked by two chairs, one of vivid red, the other of lilac. On stands and small tables scattered through the room are lamps of unusual design. On the wall right, an opened bar, its disorder displaying the abundance of alcoholic drinks in the house. Upstage a large, costly radio-phonograph with television screen. Near the sofa, a small table for a telephone, exotically decorated.

As the curtain rises on the empty room, it is about 6:30

P.M. *The lamps are lit. Everything is somewhat upset in the room, in preparation for a party. Several uncorked bottles are visible on the bar. The radio is turned on.*

RADIO: The weather is unsettled in the central zone. Some cloudiness and a few showers from Santiago southward. Weather for Santiago, Variable with probability of rain. (*The report concludes with a musical sign-off.*)

(*Enter Estela through the glass door, rear. She wears an elaborate dressing gown. As she crosses the room, she sees that the radio is turned on. She turns it off, and goes to the bar. There she examines one of the bottles, then exits right, through the dining room door.*
(*The stage remains empty for a moment, then from the dining room enter George, who has tied a coquettish apron over his shirt and trousers. He turns on the radio again, then goes out. In a moment he hurries in and dashes through the hall door, rear.*)

RADIO: Atmospheric conditions throughout the world have been very unstable since yesterday. In London, the temperature has dropped to below freezing, while in Paris a heat wave has caused heat prostration among the French. It is feared that . . .

(*Estela comes from the dining room. She is an attractive woman in the prime of life. Her movements reveal studied elegance. Because of her training as an actress, she plays a role even in real life. She is pleasant, but flighty and inconsistent.*)

ESTELA (*turning off the radio*) :   Why does somebody keep the radio going when there's nobody to listen? Isn't this house in enough uproar with this confounded cocktail party?

(*Enter Marisol, the daughter, a pretty girl, free and easy, with a certain modern air and giving evidence of what*

Estela must have been like when she was young. Marisol
is not very intelligent. She, too, wears a robe, and holds
her hands in the air, waving them to dry the finger
polish she has just applied.)

MARISOL: Cocktail party! Cocktail party! What's one more
cocktail party? (*She drops languidly onto the sofa.*)

ESTELA: Don't try to play the ingenue. You didn't inherit
my talent.

MARISOL (*ironically*): Mother, how many years ago did
you retire from the stage?

ESTELA: Ten! (*gesturing to the painting over the fireplace*)
I was smart enough to retire at the height of my glory.
Juliet was my final role and my greatest triumph.

MARISOL (*repeating from memory*): "Estela Wilson made
an unforgettable ethereal Juliet, who projected her
freshness and charm across the footlights." And at that
moment you were more than twenty years old. But
that's what the foremost theatrical critic of our era
said.

ESTELA: Not only said, but wrote. Right there on the
printed page. (*with a gesture*) So!

MARISOL: Yes, yes, Mother. You have repeated it so much
that we've hardly had any other subject of conversation
these last ten years.

ESTELA (*sternly*): Be more respectful, Marisol! Remember
you're talking to your Mother.

MARISOL: Who can't forget the theatre even when she's
talking to her daughter. But you're not Estela Wilson
the great artist, now. You're only Mrs. González with a
house to look after and in case you've forgotten it, today
we are giving a cocktail party for the Valderramas.

ESTELA: Who are your father's most important customers
with whom he expects to negotiate a deal of fifty million pesos. I know! I know! (*with a tragic theatrical*

gesture) How I hate petty domestic details! Sometimes an overpowering urge seizes me to return to the stage.

MARISOL: An urge that comes most frequently when you have problems.

ESTELA: Problems? What problems?

MARISOL: Don't you consider it a problem to give a cocktail party for fifty guests and probably twenty more who will try to crash the gate? And without a single servant to help you.

ESTELA: I couldn't stand Aurelia. She tried to perform Lope de Vega at the stove.

MARISOL: Who put it into her head that she had a talent for acting, I'd like to know.

ESTELA (*backing away*):   No, indeed, you can't blame that on me! Aurelia an actress! It was she who convinced herself that she had more inclination for the stage than for the kitchen.

MARISOL: She convinced herself because you spent day after day talking to her about plays and players, encouraging her to try to act, even while she was holding a frying pan in her hand. And before Aurelia . . . What happened to Isabel?

ESTELA (*smiling with satisfaction*):   Isabel ran away with a traveling circus, just like a novel.

MARISOL: She ran away because you told her day and night how romantic such a life was.

ESTELA: Is it my fault that such a life is romantic? (*a scornful gesture from Marisol*) Yes, I know. You don't think so. Your generation has lost all taste for art. All you're interested in is those dummies, those flat-faced comedians on a movie screen.

MARISOL: Movies are an art, Mother. The Seventh Art. That's what the movie magazines call it.

ESTELA: That's the only reading you do. Since movie stars influence fashions, you've lost all your personality. One

year you look like one star and the next year like
somebody else. Marisol, when are you going to look like
yourself?

MARISOL (*gazing at her nails*): You're dramatizing now,
Mother. Nothing in life is that important.

ESTELA: Yes, just look at those fingernails! Tropical red
because that Lollobrigida uses that color. Can't you
choose your own polish to suit your personal taste,
instead of buying one to be like those in a photograph
on a screen?

MARISOL: When you were a girl, didn't you copy your
idols?

ESTELA: Possibly. But in those days our idols were flesh and
blood, not just an animated photograph.

(*Enter Daniel, the father, through the glass door. He
wears a dressing gown. He is a big business man, pros-
perous, attractive. His business deals are not always
above board—we might say not always honorable—but
they pay big dividends.*)

DANIEL: Estela! It's happened again!

MARISOL: Oh, no, for heaven's sake!

ESTELA: What happened, dear? Your face looks like a
Greek tragic mask.

DANIEL: You know very well what I'm talking about. It
always happens when I have to dress for a formal affair.

ESTELA: Do you mean you don't have a clean dress shirt?

DANIEL: How smart you are! You're exactly right.

ESTELA: You don't need to get your blood in a boil, dear. I
left one in the first drawer of your dresser.

DANIEL (*with funereal expression*): Yes, I've just looked at
it.

ESTELA: Well, then, what are you complaining about?

DANIEL (*restraining himself with an effort*): It happens
that the shirt you left out for me is torn over one

shoulder and has ragged cuffs. It's the oldest one I own.

MARISOL: I'll bet that's the one I gave you five years ago.

DANIEL: That's the one. You can't think I'd put that one on for Eugenio Valderrama's party.

ESTELA (*falling dramatically into a chair*): Oh, what a tragedy!

DANIEL: You don't receive any guest, much less one with whom you hope to close a fifty million peso deal, in a torn shirt with ragged cuffs.

MARISOL: Daddy, you'll have to wear it. You know very well that since Aurelia dedicated herself to the Dramatic Arts, the laundress is also taking classes to keep up with her, and never gets the clothes back in time.

DANIEL (*furiously to Estela*): That's some more of your work! All your fault!

ESTELA (*innocently*): What is?

DANIEL: Stirring up the masses. Putting into their heads, first Isabel, then Aurelia, and now the laundress, that they might have a career in your damned theatre. You're nothing more or less than a communistic agitator.

ESTELA: Daniel, what an ugly word!

DANIEL: To fill the heads of people with ideas of leaving the honorable jobs they fill and running off with traveling circuses is only a form of underground communism. They ought to punish you for anti-democratic practices.

ESTELA: Stop it, Daniel! All this fuss over one insignificant matter.

DANIEL: Do you call it insignificant that I don't have a clean shirt for Eugenio Valderrama's party?

ESTELA: You do have one. Just put it on wrong side out, and nobody will notice the frayed cuffs. (*She gets up.*) Anyway, there are more important things that need my attention right now. (*She starts out.*)

DANIEL (*following her*): Listen, Estela, I . . .

MARISOL: Don't bother her about your shirt, Daddy. Mother's right. It's already six-thirty. In a half hour the guests will start arriving, and nothing is ready.

DANIEL (*to Estela*) : Do you mean to tell me that nothing's ready for the party?

ESTELA: Who do you think there was to prepare it? We haven't had a servant for at least a month.

DANIEL (*angrily*) : You could have called me at the office and I would have arranged to have everything sent out from the club.

ESTELA: I did think about it, but just as I picked up the phone, in came Adelita Goycolea and we started talking. You know how she chatters. And then it was too late.

DANIEL (*incredulously*) : Do you realize that in half an hour fifty guests will be arriving and we have nothing to feed them?

ESTELA: Oh, you're wrong! I've just sent Georgie to the liquor store to order everything. He'll be back in a minute. Then all you'll have to do is open the bottles and there you are!

DANIEL: Estela, you're out of your mind! What about food? Aren't we going to give them anything to eat?

ESTELA: I told Georgie to stop in for a tin of anchovies.

DANIEL: One can of anchovies for fifty people!

MARISOL (*starting for the door*) : They aren't going to catch me half-dressed. I've got to start making myself presentable. It usually takes me an hour and a quarter.

DANIEL: And when you're finished, what difference does it make?

MARISOL: Daddy! (*As Marisol starts out, she collides with George, who is returning from the liquor store, carrying one can of anchovies.*)

GEORGE: That girl is getting harder to live with all the time. It must be her age, that adolescent period she's reached.

DANIEL: No, son. Its just part of the general atmosphere of this house.

GEORGE: Here are the anchovies. (*Gives the can to Estela.*) The fellow at the liquor store said that's the last time he'll put up with last minute hurry-up orders, Mother. He's tired of the way you delay ordering and then expect . . .

ESTELA: That Italian is rude. I've about decided to buy our liquor somewhere else. He ought to feel honored that the former Estela Wilson is willing to drink his stuff. (*Exit in disgust carrying the can.*)

GEORGE: Mother, Mother! Thoughtless, enchanting, glamorous Mother! To her it's all a stage. But to have to live with her, that's something else again.

DANIEL: George, I forbid you to talk about your mother in those tones.

GEORGE (*paying no attention*) :   I wonder how many spectators who admire an actress on the stage would be capable of living with her day after day.

DANIEL: Not one! But speaking of problems, did anyone come here today?

GEORGE: Nobody. And I put a display ad in the paper three columns wide. It cost a fortune.

DANIEL: Servants have a keen sense of smell. They won't take a job in this house for anything in the world. Between your mother, who wants to turn them all into actresses, and your sister, who tries to handle them with the point of her toe, I'm afraid we'll have trouble finding a servant.

GEORGE: Only a miracle can bring us one.

DANIEL (*pessimistically*) :   A miracle that only Heaven could accomplish.

(*The door bell rings loud and continuously.*)

DANIEL: Sounds as if Heaven heard us.

GEORGE: Don't joke about it, father!

(The doorbell rings again. Estela appears at the dining room door.)

ESTELA: Are you deaf? Don't you hear the bell? Go and answer it, Georgie.

GEORGE *(starting)*: O.K., Mother. *(He turns at the door.)* May I remind you that we made an agreement?

ESTELA: Agreement?

GEORGE: Yes. I'm twenty years old and last week you promised from now on to call me "George." G-E-O-R-G-E. Understand? Not Georgie. *(Exit.)*

ESTELA: That boy is becoming more disagreeable every day. He's getting more and more like you.

DANIEL *(in patient tones)*: Estela, I'm going to ask you a big favor. If that's a girl at the door who has come in answer to our advertisement . . .

ESTELA *(peevishly)*: What advertisement?

DANIEL: Heavens, Estela! The one we put in *El Mercurio* for a servant,

ESTELA: Oh . . . Oh, yes.

GEORGE *(continuing)*: If that's a girl coming in answer to our advertisement, I beg you, I implore you, don't tell her she's got a good figure for the theatre.

ESTELA: But suppose she has?

DANIEL *(shouting)*: Be quiet! We need a servant, not a chorus girl.

ESTELA: Very well, Daniel. Don't shout at me. You systematically oppose all my attempts to raise the status of the laboring class. You're a typical capitalistic exploiter.

DANIEL: Thanks to which, we can all live well. I have no objection to improving the laboring class, but I don't want it done by directing them into the theatre while they're supposed to be working for us. So, I beg you, don't tell her she's a second Sarah Bernhardt.

(From the hall sounds the voice of George: "This way, please!" Enter George followed by Cecilio Paniagua.

Cecilio is about thirty-five, very correct, wearing a dark suit and suggesting by his careful manners the perfect majordomo. Only occasionally an ironical smile crosses his attractive face, as if he were gazing on an amusing spectacle—that of the world. As he enters, he pauses for an instant in the doorway. Estela and Daniel turn.)

CECILIO *(the perfect servant)* :   Mrs. González Olivo?
ESTELA: Yes.

(He sets on the floor the small valise he is carrying.)

CECILIO: May I present myself, madam. My name is Cecilio Paniagua, at your service.
ESTELA: Delighted, sir. *(She moves toward him, extending her hand. Cecilio does not take it.)* You are a little early, I'm afraid. You're one of the first. Are you a friend of the Valderramas?
GEORGE *(trying to interrupt)* :   Mother, this gentleman is . . .
ESTELA: Don't tell me. You must be related to the Valderramas. That family likeness is unmistakable.
DANIEL: Estela, I think you're making a mistake.
ESTELA *(peevishly)* :   I never make a mistake. I'm an expert physiognomist.
GEORGE: This gentleman is not a guest, Mother.
ESTELA *(still more peevish)* :   If he isn't a guest, what is he doing at our cocktail party?
GEORGE: He has come in answer to our advertisement.
CECILIO: Yes, madam, your advertisement in *El Mercurio*. I thought it was beautiful and appealing! A request for a servant that sprang from the heart. "Here's a desperate family," I told myself. "A family like millions on this wretched asteroid called earth."

(All stare at him. His words sound strange. Estela reacts.)

ESTELA: How beautiful! You talk exactly like someone accustomed to the theatre, Mr . . . Mr. . . .

CECILIO: Cecilio Paniagua, at your service.

ESTELA: I'll call you Ceci. How does that sound? I think it just fits you. Ceci!

CECILIO: Delighted, madam.

ESTELA: Very well, then, Ceci. We're not one of the common run of families because I, the mother, am a great actress, Estela Wilson, of whom you've doubtless heard.

GEORGE: Small correction. She *was* a great actress. Now she's been retired for ten years. So it's pluperfect tense.

ESTELA: Don't pay any attention to him, Ceci. My son and my husband, since they don't appreciate art, look down on it. But you, who are certainly a sensitive person, must understand that the theatrical art is. . . .

DANIEL (*interrupting her*): Estela, let's concentrate on the main thing. Paniagua, you wish employment in what capacity?

CECILIO: I've never been employed but He insisted that it is the best way to proceed in such cases. Especially when dealing with mortals.

DANIEL (*completely mystified*): I'm afraid I don't understand a word of what you're saying.

CECILIO (*quickly recovering*): Excuse me. I was only reflecting to myself, a defect that Mrs. González, like the great actress that she is, will certainly forgive. (*He bows slightly to her.*) I'm afraid I'm given to reflecting aloud.

DANIEL: That's all right, if it isn't too loud.

CECILIO: No, no, sir. Besides, I'll try to control this defect when I enter into service.

GEORGE: Splendid!

DANIEL: What sort of employment are you looking for?

CECILIO: Whatever you have to offer, sir.

GEORGE: That's an ambiguous reply!

DANIEL: What I meant to say was, what do you know how to do?

CECILIO: Do, sir?

DANIEL: Yes; cook, clean, wax, iron, valet, etc.

CECILIO (*nodding*) : Oh, yes. I had forgotten that for you people, those are important details. I can do them all.

GEORGE: All?

CECILIO (*with great naturalness*) : Yes, and besides, I know how to prepare delicious nectar and ambrosia.

DANIEL (*surprised*) : I don't believe they will be needed for the moment.

CECILIO (*to Estela*) : Oh, I don't agree with your husband, madam. In cocktail parties where I come from, they're the fashionable drink.

ESTELA: We'll try them one of these days, Ceci. I suppose they're new drinks. People give them all such unusual names nowadays.

GEORGE (*suspicious*) : You said: "Where I come from." What does that mean?

CECILIO (*ready with a quick lie*) : I meant in England, sir. I used to be employed in the household of Lord Baslow in Mayfair.

ESTELA: Oh, an English majordomo! The ambition of my life. You must come and work for us, Ceci.

CECILIO: Those are my intentions, madam.

DANIEL: You'll be supplied with all sorts of conveniences, a sunny room with private bath . . .

GEORGE: It's only a shower.

CECILIO (*uncomprehending*) : Shower? Oh, yes, that North American invention that up there we call rain. I won't use it.

ESTELA: Don't you like shower baths?

CECILIO: We're not accustomed to bathing, madam. That's just one of your affectations.

GEORGE: Well! I didn't know the English felt that way.

ESTELA: But isn't that rather inconvenient, especially in summer? I suppose you use a deodorant.

CECILIO: No, all I need is to fan myself.

GEORGE: What extraordinary customs!

DANIEL: Now about the salary . . .

CECILIO: Don't worry about that, sir. That's not of the least importance.

DANIEL: I like that man!

ESTELA: Don't listen to my husband. We are accustomed to paying our servants very well.

GEORGE: Mother's right. Sometimes they earn so much that, added to what they get away with, they live extremely well on their income.

CECILIO *(to himself)* :   He was right when He assured me that being a domestic employee on earth is big business, with identity card, free medical care, social security, and everything.

DANIEL: You're right.

CECILIO: But you must understand, sir, that I'm not interested in a salary because, we . . . well, we don't pay any attention to money.

ESTELA: Really? You must belong to the Salvation Army.

CECILIO: Yes, I guess you could say I belong to an army that might be called "salvation," if madam likes.

ESTELA: I like people with firm religious convictions. Of course for me, my real religion is the theatre. You and I, Ceci . . .

DANIEL: Estela!

ESTELA: All right! All right! *(to Cecilio)* Later, by ourselves, we can discuss art. My husband is interested only in the commercial world. But I feel, Ceci, that you have a sensitive soul that understands art and especially the theatre.

CECILIO: Some, madam, some. I've always been interested in the Human Comedy. You might say I've looked at it from a gallery seat. One can see it better from there.

ESTELA: Oh, my public in the gallery! The best and most faithful in the world. How I miss them!

DANIEL: Paniagua, in forty minutes we're supposed to be

giving a cocktail party for Eugenio Valderrama, with whom I hope to sign a fifty million peso contract. So far, there's nothing ready.

ESTELA: How can you say that, Daniel? We have a can of anchovies and we've put in an order at the liquor store. Do you call that nothing?

CECILIO: Don't worry, madam! I'll attend to the party. I'm an expert in such matters. Whenever He gave a party, the only angel he ever called on was me.

GEORGE (*quickly*): Angel?

CECILIO (*recovering*): Oh, yes. In England they call the especially reliable servants "angels." It's a tradition dating back to the time of Queen Victoria.

ESTELA: How nice! I adore traditions. (*smiling*) And are you classified as an angel, Ceci?

CECILIO (*with a gleam in his eyes*): Only of the third category, madam. For special jobs. To tell the truth, there, like here, one needs pull and influence to get ahead. It's the same everywhere.

DANIEL: Naturally. That's the price we must pay for democracy.

CECILIO: So now if you will tell me where the kitchen and the pantry are, I can start getting ready for the cocktail party.

ESTELA: Georgie, show Ceci the rest of the house.

GEORGE (*going to the door*): This way, Paniagua.

CECILIO (*picking up his valise*): If you'll excuse me . . .

ESTELA: Yes, go right ahead, Ceci.

GEORGE: You've got a lot of work ahead, Paniagua. Aurelia left the kitchen in a frightful mess.

CECILIO: Don't worry, sir. I've got invisible hands to help me (*smiles*) in a manner of speaking, of course. (*Cecilio bows to them and follows George through the glass door, rear.*)

ESTELA: How delightful! My intuition never fails. What an extraordinary man!

DANIEL: Just what I was thinking. There is something extraordinary about him, a certain air of mystery.

ESTELA: A certain attractiveness, charm . . . He's fascinating. What a pleasant man!

DANIEL: Maybe, but . . .

ESTELA: But what?

DANIEL: I don't know. It's only a feeling, that's all. While we were talking, I had a feeling he was observing us.

ESTELA: Of course he was observing us, since he was looking right at us.

DANIEL: Oh, Estela, you don't understand what I mean. I'm not referring to that.

ESTELA: Then what are you referring to, dear?

DANIEL: I don't know. Something vague, inexplicable. As if he were talking to us and at the same time weighing our words and judging our actions.

ESTELA: Don't be silly! He's the perfect majordomo. I think we have found a treasure in Ceci.

DANIEL: Well, maybe. We'll see. However, you won't deny that some of the things he said sounded strange. Cocktail parties with nectar and ambrosia! And such vague references. First he'd say one thing and then the opposite. I was a bit upset.

ESTELA: All English majordomos are upsetting. Everybody knows that. It's obvious you never performed in an English comedy.

(*Enter George.*)

GEORGE: I left him in the kitchen. Would you believe that he lit the gas stove with his finger?

ESTELA: How?

GEORGE: He turned the knob, let the gas flow for a moment, then when he made some gesture with his index finger, the stove was lit, believe it or not.

ESTELA: Georgie, you got a drink at the liquor store! You know very well I don't allow that.

GEORGE: Mother, I swear that's what he did. I saw it with my own eyes.

ESTELA: Don't take your mother for a fool. Lighting the stove with his index finger! Even a sorcerer couldn't do that.

DANIEL *(slowly)*: Maybe that is what he is. That man may be a sorcerer.

(Enter Marisol, elegantly dressed for the party. She is very lovely.)

MARISOL: Who? Who are you talking about?

ESTELA: Your father, as usual, is rambling. Then he accuses me of being fantastic and theatrical.

DANIEL *(thoughtfully)*: There's something strange about that man. *(He starts toward the door.)* And I'm going to investigate right now. *(As he passes her, Estela grabs him firmly.)*

ESTELA: You are not! The only time we've ever had the chance to hire a good servant, a perfect English major-domo, I won't let you drive him away by interfering.

DANIEL: But, Estela . . .

ESTELA *(disregarding him)*: You know very well how touchy servants are these days. If you want, you can take it out on me. But don't you touch servants with even a rose petal. They're too hard to get.

DANIEL: That's the limit! Even in our own house, a person can't question a servant.

ESTELA *(looking at her wrist watch)*: Whee! I've hardly got time to get dressed. Come, Daniel. You've got to help me zip up my black dress. It always gets caught.

DANIEL *(in bad humor)*: I wasn't planning to get dressed. I don't have any clean shirt. *(He sits down stubbornly.)*

ESTELA: Are you going to receive the Valderramas, looking like that?

DANIEL *(slyly)*: Exactly. That'll show them the kind of woman I married.

(Enter Cecilio at rear door. In his hands is a spotlessly clean white shirt, beautifully ironed.)

CECILIO *(casually)* : Here's your white shirt, sir.

DANIEL: What?

CECILIO: I took the liberty of washing and ironing it, sir.

DANIEL: When?

CECILIO: A moment ago.

DANIEL: Why, that's impossible! You couldn't have had time.

CECILIO *(handing the shirt to Daniel who takes it cautiously)* : For me, nothing is impossible, sir. I have my ways. *(Exit Cecilio in silence. A pause follows.)*

MARISOL *(gazing after him in ecstacy)* : He's marvelous. What a man! He doesn't seem to walk. He floats.

DANIEL *(staring at the shirt)* : He's a sorcerer. That shirt . . . It must be sorcery.

ESTELA: Heavens, Daniel, are you never satisfied? You complained because you didn't have a clean shirt, and now that you have one, you still complain. There's no way of satisfying you. *(a theatrical gesture)* Wives . . . wives . . . the eternal martyrs! *(Exit, dramatically.)*

DANIEL *(still holding the shirt)* : He's a sorcerer. There's no doubt about it. *(He goes out as though hypnotized by the shirt.)*

GEORGE *(looking at Marisol)* : Be careful, sister of mine. I know what you're up to. Watch those sticky fingers.

MARISOL: I don't know what you're talking about.

GEORGE: When you get that expression of a hungry cat in your eyes, it means you've got your claws bared for somebody.

MARISOL: I shall ignore your vulgarity, GEORGIE!

GEORGE *(furious)* : Don't you call me Georgie or I'll choke you.

MARISOL: Heavens, what a temper! I'm sorry for the woman who marries you. When are you going to learn to control yourself? You're not a baby any more, remember?

GEORGE: Maybe I have my faults, but at least my sex impulses are under control.

MARISOL (*losing her poise*):   What do you mean by that vulgarity?

GEORGE: I don't go running after the majordomo of a house.

MARISOL: If you did, dear, it would seem to me a bit too much.

GEORGE (*at the door*):   And I'd advise you not to try it, either.

MARISOL: Why not? He's an attractive man with good manners and he's past thirty, just the sort of man I like.

GEORGE: Yes? Well, maybe Mother could take it to have you chasing him, but she'd never stand your frightening him away. Remember that! (*Exit George quickly.*)

MARISOL (*angrily*):   Elephant!

(*She goes to a box of cigarettes and lights one. As she puffs, she paces the floor, scowling in thought. Finally making up her mind, she goes to the dining room door and calls.*)

MARISOL: Hey, you! Come here!

(*After a pause, as the girl continues to pace nervously, enter Cecilio.*)

CECILIO: Did the señorita call me?

MARISOL: Yes. What's your name?

CECILIO: Cecilio Paniagua, at your service, señorita.

MARISOL: Cecilio . . . Cecilio . . . What a funny name. I'm going to call you Ce.

CECILIO: You keep shortening my name. Your mother baptized me Ceci, and now you call me Ce. If we keep on at this rate, I'll end up being only a hiss.

MARISOL: So what? I like Ce, so I'll call you Ce.

CECILIO: Whatever gives you pleasure, señorita.

MARISOL: Really? Oh, fine! I like to have men anxious to give me pleasure. And I might add that I never lack men.

CECILIO (*looking at her*) :   Oh, I'm sure of that.

MARISOL: They adore me. Platonically, of course, but it's still adoration.

CECILIO: Congratulations.

MARISOL (*repeating the name as if it were music*) :   Ce . . . Ce, Ce. That's poetic. It has a certain musical ring. Don't you think so?

CECILIO: If you say so, though down here you have a different sense of music than we do.

MARISOL: What are you talking about? What do you mean?

CECILIO: Your music has more variety and it is certainly noisier. Mambos, sambas, rock-and-roll! Now our music, where I come from, is still in the period of the harp. Everything is accompanied by the harp. I might even call it our national instrument.

MARISOL: The harp?

CECILIO: Yes, it's soft, slow, and heavenly!

MARISOL: How boring!

CECILIO: You're right, señorita! There, too, among the young people, there's a movement to eliminate the harp, especially for dancing.

MARISOL (*with a sudden inspiration*) :   Do you know, Ce, I'm going to teach you a new dance. *She goes toward the console to put on a record.*)

CECILIO: Oh, no, señorita!

MARISOL (*starting the music*) :   Come on, man. Don't look like that! I'm not going to eat you. (*She extends her arms. Cecilio backs around the sofa.*)

CECILIO: No! Impossible. We're forbidden to touch . . . (*He stops, realizing that he was about to reveal something, and changes the phrase.*) We servants are forbidden to become intimate with our employers. That was firmly impressed on me in England.

MARISOL: I like to know everybody intimately. (*She follows him. He backs away.*)

CECILIO: Please, señorita! Your parents might come in. (*He gets to the phonograph and shuts it off.*)

MARISOL: So you don't want to dance with me, Ce?

CECILIO: I'd be happy to learn that dance if you stay in one corner of the room and I in another.

MARISOL: Don't be foolish, man! That's what dances are for . . . So people can get together. Come!

CECILIO: Impossible! Does the señorita require me for anything else?

MARISOL (*approaching insinuatingly*) :   Nothing. I just want us to get to know each other better. That's all.

CECILIO: Well, now that we know each other . . . if it's all the same to you, I'll go back to . . . (*He starts toward the dining room, but Marisol steps in front of him, blocking the door.*)

MARISOL: But it's not the same, Ce, not at all the same.

CECILIO: Señorita, please! May I go back to the kitchen?

MARISOL: Not yet. (*Advances toward him.*) Tell me, Ce, how do you like me?

CECILIO (*pretending not to understand*) :   What do you mean?

MARISOL: I mean, how do you like me? Come, man, I'm interested in your opinion of me. What do you think of me as a woman?

CECILIO (*swallowing*) :   Well, I . . . That is . . . I'll tell you some day.

MARISOL (*peremptorily*) :   No, now! Do you think I'm attractive?

CECILIO (*without conviction*) :   Yes . . . Very.

MARISOL: Well, then, why don't you make love to me?

CECILIO: Please, señorita.

MARISOL: You think I'm attractive, don't you?

CECILIO: Yes. . . .

MARISOL: Splendid!

CECILIO: Attractive, but a bit incomplete.

MARISOL (*alarmed*) : Incomplete? Do you mean I lack something?

CECILIO: Exactly!

MARISOL: Well, nobody has ever told me that before. They've assured me I'm fine the way I am. That I possess all I need, not too much or too little.

CECILIO (*almost to himself*) : There's no doubt, for the tastes of these people, she's not bad. But with a pair of detachable wings she'd be much more attractive.

MARISOL (*astonished*) : Wings? Did you say a pair of wings?

CECILIO (*coming back to reality*) : Oh, excuse me! My mind was wandering. I wasn't here at all.

MARISOL (*looking at him skeptically*) : Tell me, Ce, are you sure you're all here up here? (*touching her head*)

CECILIO: Oh, yes, señorita. Absolutely. If I weren't, I wouldn't be here. They're very strict up there. We have to take a complete physical before we're sent on any important mission. We get a complete X-ray, too.

MARISOL (*staring at him*) : Up there? Mission? What the devil are you talking about?

CECILIO: Please, señorita, don't name "the other." (*catching himself up*) Excuse me. I keep forgetting that you people aren't brought up on business principles. I was referring to England, where we are trained to serve in even minor details.

MARISOL: Oh, that's it? (*coming closer*) Listen, Ce. Do you know you're a very fascinating man?

CECILIO: Oh, the señorita exaggerates.

MARISOL (*more insinuating*) : And before Mónica Donoso steals you away, I want to get my hands on you. So let's get back to the main topic of conversation.

CECILIO (*drawing back*) : I'd just as soon not get back to the main topic of conversation.

MARISOL: Why not? Don't you enjoy it?

CECILIO: Quite the contrary, señorita.

MARISOL: Because you don't like women? If that's the trouble tell me right out and we'll be as good friends as ever. I have a number of acquaintances like that. They're silly, the poor fellows.

CECILIO: That's not it, either.

MARISOL: Then what is the trouble?

CECILIO: The trouble is our Code of Rules of Conduct, paragraph 5, section 3.

MARISOL: Now you're not making sense again. I don't understand one word of it.

CECILIO: Section 3 of paragraph 5 of our Rules of Conduct absolutely forbids certain intimacies with those down here.

MARISOL: Huh?

CECILIO *(catching himself)* :   It says an employee is not permitted certain intimacies with his employer.

MARISOL: That's silly, Ce. This is the Age of Socialism. We're all equal. (*She approaches him, but again he escapes her touch.*)

CECILIO: Oh, no, señorita! I'm not equal to everybody else. The error you mortals make is to think that someday everybody will be equal. It's a pure illusion.

MARISOL *(not listening)* :   Kiss me!

CECILIO: No!

MARISOL: Do you refuse?

CECILIO: I'm thinking it over.

MARISOL: You're thinking it over!

CECILIO: Whether it would be right to disobey paragraph 5, section 3. (*decisively*) No! No, it's too risky. They'd send me down, and it's hellishly hot down there. (*He moves away from her.*)

MARISOL: A man who refuses to kiss me! Unheard of. (*She goes up to him and boxes his ears, loudly.*) Insolent! To dare to refuse me. And nothing but a simple servant.

(Exit, slamming the door.)

CECILIO: How strange the virgins are down here. They get angry because someone won't kiss them. It's quite the opposite up there. *(He goes to the radio and turns it on.)*

RADIO: Weather predictions still remain unsettled. All over the planet atmospheric changes are occurring that greatly puzzle the scientists of America, Europe, Asia, Africa, and Oceania.

(The voice over the radio, to which Cecilio has been listening with an ironic smile, fades away. A silence follows. Then a roaring sound is heard, followed by several thunder claps. At once Cecilio stands in an expectant attitude in front of it. One might think he was a soldier about to receive orders from his commander. New thunderclaps in the radio.)

CECILIO: Yes, Lord. I'm carrying out the mission you assigned to me. *(several thunder-claps)* No, I still haven't made much progress. I took a position in the González house. Yes, a typical family. You who sees all and knows all, must know them. *(thunder)* Just what I thought. Your opinion of them isn't very flattering. *(thunder)* What? You've ordered St. Peter to provide a beautiful spring day! . . . Well, if You want my opinion, and not because I want to meddle in Your affairs, because they're already too muddled . . . *(loud thunder)* No, don't get angry! All I wanted to say is that tomorrow it ought to rain bucketfuls with a fall of lava and thunder and lightning. You know very well that tomorrow as it is written . . . *(furious thunder)* Forgive me, Lord. I had forgotten that You wrote it. Yes, I know You are the boss. Yes, Your will be done. *(gentler thunder)* Of course, Lord. I'll follow exactly the directions concerning my mission here below. *(thunder)* Tomorrow I'll begin the second step. I'll start the examinations. Is that all right? (*continuous thunder*) Very well. I'll do it. I'll do everything. Don't worry, Lord. Yes, Lord. Goodbye until tomorrow. (*He turns off the radio and as he goes toward the kitchen he mutters*) Why did He ever decide to provide a sunny day for tomorrow? He's so capricious. No wonder people down here sometimes call Him Destiny. (*as he goes out*)

CURTAIN

ACT 2

The same setting, the following morning. As the curtain rises, the stage is empty, though there are still a few evidences of the cocktail party, with bottles and glasses on the tables. In a moment enter Cecilio with tray containing coffee and rolls for four. He puts the tray on the center table. At that moment, the door opens. Enter Estela in an elegant morning dress.

ESTELA:　Good morning, Ceci. (*Goes to the window and looks out.*) What a splendid morning!

CECILIO:　Good morning, madam.

ESTELA:　This sun is awful for my aching head. Oooh! I feel as if it would split.

CECILIO:　Perhaps if madam would take some black coffee . . .

ESTELA:　Are you suggesting, Ceci, that I have a hangover?

CECILIO:　Oh, no, I'd never dare suggest anything like that. I'm sure you took only a little gin to celebrate the triumph.

ESTELA:　A triumph entirely due to you, Ceci. The party turned out very successful. The drinks were perfect. The snacks couldn't have been more delicious. But what I wonder is, how you could have got it all ready so well and in so short a time.

CECILIO (*enigmatically*) :   I have my resources, madam.

ESTELA: The Valderramas were astonished. After four of those dry martinis that you mixed so well, Eugenio Valderrama signed the contract with George without blinking. Fifty million!

(*Enter Daniel in excellent humor, dressed in an elegant morning jacket.*)

DANIEL: Good morning! Good morning! (*He kisses Estela on the cheek.*) Good morning, dear. (*Goes to the window.*) What a beautiful day!

CECILIO: Good morning, sir. Coffee or tea?

DANIEL: Cecilio! (*approaching him affectionately*)   My dear Cecilio, you are my angel of salvation!

CECILIO (*smiling to himself*) :   The angel part of that is, of course, only your kindness.

DANIEL: No, I mean it. Last night you made it possible for me to close one of the most important negotiations of my career. You are an angel!

CECILIO (*still smiling*) :   I've been called that before.

ESTELA: What's the matter?

CECILIO: Nothing, madam. I was thinking aloud. It's a deep-seated custom of mine.

DANIEL (*sitting beside Estela*) :   Darling, with this business concluded, our old age is secure. No worries for the rest of our lives.

CECILIO (*to himself, pouring their coffee*) :   Which may be shorter than you think.

ESTELA (*looking at him*) :   There is something wrong, Ceci. You're very strange. You talk to yourself all the time.

CECILIO: Overwork, I guess, Madam.

ESTELA (*pensively*) :   Yes, that might be it.

(*Enter Marisol in morning dress or slacks. She is in a peevish humor.*)

MARISOL: Good morning to everybody . . . (*She kisses her parents.*) . . . except one.

ESTELA: Marisol, what do you mean by such an absurd remark?

MARISOL: I mean I refuse to wish Ce a good morning.

ESTELA: Ce?

DANIEL: That's what she has been calling him since last night. She considers Cecilio too long, so just as you shortened it to Ceci . . .

CECILIO: Coffee or tea, señorita?

MARISOL (*turning her head away*): Poison, good and strong.

ESTELA: Marisol! I've told you a thousand times! You must treat the help kindly. That's a sign of good breeding.

MARISOL: When someone offends me as deeply as he did, then . . . (*She makes a gesture toward Cecilio.*)

ESTELA: Offend? Did you offend her, Ceci?

CECILIO: If madam permits, I don't wish to discuss the matter. I have a hard day ahead and I don't wish to tire myself prematurely with trivial discussions.

MARISOL: Cretin!

(*Enter George in sweater and slacks.*)

GEORGE: I see that we've started the day well with my darling sister, as usual, uttering sweet words. (*He kisses his parents.*) Good morning, Mother; Good morning, Father.

ESTELA: Good morning, precious.

GEORGE: What a huge success last night! And that miracle was entirely due to you, Cecilio.

CECILIO: Thanks, George. Tea or coffee?

GEORGE: Coffee, please, and plenty strong. I'm afraid I was a bit heavy-handed with the cognac last night.

DANIEL: Everybody drank too much last night. Some, cognac; some . . . (*looking at Estela*) gin.

ESTELA: I don't know what you mean. (*to Cecilio*) Have the morning papers come yet, Ceci?

CECILIO (*hesitating and not giving them to her*): Yes, they're here, madam.

ESTELA: Well, let me see them. I want to read the news.

CECILIO (*still holding them*):   I'd rather you didn't, madam. Wouldn't it be better to listen to it on radio?

DANIEL: What do you mean?

CECILIO: I'm sure Chileans will find the news in the paper this morning surprising and disagreeable. And since I've grown fond of them, I'd like to delay the bad moment.

GEORGE: What are you talking about?

MARISOL: He's crazier than a goat! I realized that yesterday. Only a crazy man could scorn me.

DANIEL: I demand that you explain those strange words, Cecilio.

CECILIO: It's better for you to learn about it on radio, sir.

(*Daniel goes to the radio, then stops.*)

DANIEL: Learn about it on radio? What do you mean?

CECILIO: All the stations in Chile are having simultaneous transmission about the event, by government orders.

ESTELA: What event?

DANIEL (*at the radio*):   I'll turn it on.

(*He is about to do so, but Estela stops him.*)

ESTELA (*suspiciously*):   No, Daniel, don't turn it on. Let Ceci tell us what it's all about. He seems well informed about it . . . too well informed. (*She gets up and faces Cecilio.*) Who are you?

CECILIO (*as if repeating something memorized*):   I am Cecilio Paniagua, the model servant, at your service, madam.

MARISOL (*going to him*):   Aha! There's something crooked going on. Yesterday after our little scene, I stopped behind the door and listened . . .

ESTELA: Marisol! You listened behind doors? How horrible!

MARISOL: Yes, I listened and I overheard the strangest conversation I've ever heard in my life. This man was talking with the radio.

GEORGE: Sister, you have a worse hangover than I thought. Nobody talks *with* a radio. Men talk on the radio.

MARISOL: Not this man! The radio replied to him.

DANIEL: What did it say to him? What did it say?

MARISOL: It sounded like thunder, a sort of repeated thunderclap with some hidden meaning. He listened very carefully. (*All stand, staring at Cecilio.*)

ESTELA: Cecilio, explain all this. Explain it, right away! Is what my daughter said true?

CECILIO (*calmly*): Yes, madam, it's quite true.

DANIEL: Do you mean you were conversing with the radio?

CECILIO: It's the quickest means of communication we have from down here. We always use it to report the results of a mission.

GEORGE: Wait a minute! What do you mean, down here?

CECILIO: I'm referring to this planet, to the earth.

ESTELA: I'm afraid I'm going crazy! Completely crazy. I don't understand a word. You aren't an inhabitant of Mars, are you, Ceci?

CECILIO: Oh, no, madam. Much farther away than that.

DANIEL: Farther away? Explain yourself. Who are you? Answer me this instant or I'll call the police.

CECILIO: I'm afraid the police could do little about it, sir.

ALL (*in unison*): Who are you?

(*There is a pause. Cecilio moves to the center of the room.*)

CECILIO: I am Exterminating Angel XM 26 (*modestly*) Just barely in the third category. (*general consternation*)

ESTELA (*slowly*): An angel? You? Impossible! You don't

look like an angel. You don't have that beatified air. In the theatre, it's always possible to recognize an angel. They wear white. I know because once I was an angel in a play. I had a marvelous white costume.

CECILIO: The theatre has nothing to do with reality, madam. It is—well, you might say—more real than reality. Besides, times have changed, madam. Today we angels have our own unions. We're sophisticated, ingenious, even existentialists. We know how to make very dry martinis and we read Sartre, Grahame Green, and Noel Coward. That's the way we are educated in the Angels' High School. Otherwise, how could we expect to be successful when we come down to earth on a mission?

ESTELA: I don't believe it. I refuse to believe it.

GEORGE: What about your wings? When I was young, I learned to identify angels in pictures and on altars. They always had wings. Where are yours?

CECILIO: In my room, sir, in the small black valise I carry with me.

DANIEL: You mean you put them on and off the way women use gloves?

CECILIO: Why not, sir? They're the latest model, made of waterproof nylon and equipped with jet propulsion. They were designed by Christian . . . Dior. They're very chic.

ESTELA: One of these days you've got to let me model them, Ceci. How envious Saruca Aguirre will be when she sees me wearing wings.

MARISOL: Mother! (*to Cecilio*) I don't believe a word of all that man has told us. How do you know he's an angel? Just because he says so? How easy that would be, just like my telling you that I'm a witch.

GEORGE: Don't ever say that, darling sister! People might easily believe you.

MARISOL (*to them all*): How can you be so gullible? What

proof has he given us that he is really an angel? Now, if
God had sent him . . .

CECILIO *(interrupting her)* : Just a minute, señorita! Let's
not involve the Lord in this. You mortals are always
invoking Him. And I warn you that He doesn't like it.
Up there we have more respect for our Boss. Why, do
you know, angels of the fifth category haven't even seen
him.

MARISOL: Nonsense! I repeat I've got to have proofs before
I believe this man. *(She approaches Cecilio threateningly.)* Yes, proofs! And if you can't produce a few in a
hurry, you and your nylon wings can go flying off
somewhere else!

ESTELA *(coquettishly)* : But he does have a rather angelic
face. Doesn't that convince you, Marisol?

CECILIO: Very well, if the señorita insists. I was trying to
spare you this, but *(handing the newspaper to Estela)*
there's your proof. Right on the front page.

*(All gather around Estela as she unfolds the newspaper
and gazes hypnotized at the front page.)*

ESTELA *(after a pause)* : What a good picture, Ceci. That's
cute!

CECILIO *(modestly)* : Thank you, madam.

MARISOL *(reading)* : "The first angel ever to visit Chile.
Exclusive interview with Cecilio Paniagua, who arrived
in our nation yesterday from Heaven, sent on a special
mission."

CECILIO: May I point out to the señorita that I have a
higher rating than Marilyn Monroe. The reporter calls
me "The Man of the Century."

MARISOL *(continuing to read)* : "Cecilio Paniagua, Exterminating Angel XM 26, third category, refused yesterday upon arrival at the Santiago airport under his own
wings, to give details of the mission that brings him to
Chile. All he would say to the hundreds of reporters

from different publications in the capital who kept questioning him, was: 'I am very happy to visit this asteroid. It is my first time here in this role. My purpose is to examine at first hand a typical Chilean family, as one might say, in their own surroundings. Concerning the purpose of my visit, I cannot give you details yet, since it involves a professional secret that He does not want discussed. Finally I am grateful to the press for its interest in me. Up there, the Yankees have taught us the value of publicity. Thank you.' Then adjusting his nylon wings, the angel Cecilio Paniagua disappeared from before our astonished eyes."

DANIEL: Incredible! To think that a serious paper like *El Mercurio,* generally so well-informed, would publish a yarn like that!

ESTELA: I don't like that remark about our being a typical Chilean family, Ceci. Why didn't you tell them you were visiting the home of the most famous actress of Chile's theatre?

CECILIO: I *do* apologize, madam. It was an oversight, I assure you.

GEORGE: But we still don't know the reason for this unexplained visit, Cecilio. Will you be kind enough to explain?

CECILIO: If you had bothered to turn on the radio this morning, you would have had that explanation.

DANIEL: What does the radio have to do with all this?

CECILIO: I've already told you, sir, the government network has been broadcasting about the event ever since early this morning.

ESTELA: Still, it doesn't seem very courteous for those up there to be sending angels down here without being invited.

DANIEL: Hush, Estela! (*to Cecilio*) What event? Why have you come among us, Cecilio? What's your purpose?

CECILIO (*casually*): It's the Last Judgment, sir.

ESTELA: Last Judgment?

MARISOL: Last Judgment?

DANIEL: Last Judgment?

GEORGE: What are you talking about?

CECILIO *(still casual)* :   Today's the day.

ESTELA: The day? What day?

CECILIO: The Day of the Last Judgment.

ESTELA: My God!

CECILIO: Don't name Him, madam! He doesn't like it.

DANIEL *(thunderstruck)* :   The Day of the Last Judgment! Devil take me!

CECILIO: It's quite possible your wish will be fulfilled, sir.

MARISOL: Stop joking, Ce!

CECILIO: It's no joke, señorita. Everything I've said is absolutely true. Today is the Day of the Last Judgment.

MARISOL: You're a humbug, Ce. Today can't be the Day of the Last Judgment. Both the Old and the New Testament are very clear about details. The Last Judgment will be heralded by burning mountains, floods, and all sorts of catastrophes. This is a beautiful sunny day.

GEORGE *(at the window)* :   Yes, Cecilio. Look out there. My sister is absolutely right. It's an unusually beautiful day for this time of year.

CECILIO: Yes, I know. That's another whim of the Lord. Sometimes His whims go beyond the bounds of logic.

ESTELA: It's not fair. It's just not fair! I refuse to believe the Last Judgment can take place in full sunlight. It's not dramatic. It will lose all its effectiveness. Your Boss ought to hire a theatre director.

DANIEL: Theatre, theatre! All you think of is theatre. Even on the Day of the Last Judgment.

CECILIO: Didn't someone declare, sir, that life is a play? And speaking of plays, I suppose that from now on all of you will realize you are under examination.

GEORGE: Examination? Like those in the university?

CECILIO: More or less. Except that this time it's your life

that's being examined. That makes it a bit more important, doesn't it? You and all the population of the other
Latin American countries are being examined today. By
now, many thousands of angels have descended to earth
to begin the inventory.

DANIEL: Inventory? What sort of inventory?

CECILIO: Of your sins, naturally. You'll be graded by that.
And it will be decided whether you'll go to Heaven,
Limbo, or . . . to the other place.

ESTELA: Not me! I'm not going to Limbo. I can't stand
those stage waits. Waiting in the wings has always been
torture to me. Worse than a dentist's waiting room.

CECILIO: I'm afraid, madam, that this time you have little
to say about the choice. Orders from higher up, you
know.

GEORGE (*rebelliously*) :   Suppose we object and don't obey?

CECILIO (*calmly*) :   In that case you'll simply disappear,
disintegrate, cease to be. You'll be reintegrated into
nothingness out of which you were created.

ESTELA: How horrible! I won't accept the conditions, Ceci.
Nothingness is all right for Sartre, but it doesn't attract
me at all.

CECILIO: Don't worry, madam. Quite likely you'll all pass
the examination brilliantly. And in that case . . .

ALL (*together*) :   In that case, what?

CECILIO: Well, in that case, you'll enjoy eternal grace, celestial bliss, and you'll go to Heaven.

MARISOL: Heaven? Where you came from, Ce?

CECILIO: That's right, señorita.

MARISOL: That doesn't sound so attractive, either. If all the
men there are like you, I don't believe I'd enjoy it
much.

ESTELA: Marisol! All that girl thinks of is men!

MARISOL: What else do you want me to think of, Mother?

DANIEL: Stop it! Such discussions are futile. The time has
come to put our lives onto the scales. That's no light

thing. It's serious, very serious. Who's in charge of the examination, Cecilio?

GEORGE: Don't tell me that another angel is going to fly down to our house. That's more than I could take!

(*A sudden clap of thunder. All are startled, except Cecilio.*)

ESTELA: There it is. We're going to have a rain shower of angels. Go and open the door, Georgie.

(*George starts out, but Cecilio stops him.*)

CECILIO: Just a minute, sir. I'll open it. I think it's for me.

(*Exit Cecilio. The moment he leaves, the four on stage talk rapidly and nervously.*)

ESTELA: What a nightmare! The Day of the Last Judgment. Daniel, do you believe they'll take into account the bad things I've said about Adelita Rodríguez? If they do, I'm sunk.

DANIEL: And that stock in the Unlucky Mine that I falsified. I wonder if they know about that.

GEORGE: Will they hold against me the way I cheated in the final examinations for graduation?

MARISOL: You and your childish problems! What worries me is whether they'll think it was a sin to steal Nené Guzmán's fiancé. I think myself it was a good deed.

ESTELA (*seized by a sudden idea*):   I know! We'll forget all our sins. All we'll tell are our good deeds.

DANIEL: Don't you realize, Estela, that would be a lie? You'd just be adding one more sin to the already long list.

ESTELA: One swallow doesn't make a summer, and one more little sin surely wouldn't condemn me to . . . to that other place.

GEORGE: Mother, surely he'll realize that we are lying. He

must already know our sins. He comes from up there
where they set down everything we do on earth.

ESTELA: If he knows everything, why does he come down
here to question us?

DANIEL: Maybe to make comparisons.

ESTELA: Nonsense! He isn't God. He's just an angel of the
third category, what you might call a supporting actor.
Therefore he can't know much.

(*Enter Cecilio, carrying a handful of blanks.*)

CECILIO (*holding them*) :   Your questionnaires.

ESTELA: Do we have to fill them in like income tax blanks?

DANIEL: If they're very complicated, you'll have to give me
time to send for my lawyer. I've never been able to fill
in those things.

CECILIO: I must apologize for these documents. But up
there, just like down here, they have to give the government employees something to do. (*He distributes them
and they leaf through the questionnaires.*) Now if
there's any question you don't understand, I beg of you
to ask me for an explanation.

(*They all sit down. There is a pause as they concentrate
on the study of the document.*)

ESTELA: There's something here I don't understand . . .
(*Reads.*) "Tell whether you have ever committed a
carnal sin or not." Just exactly what does that mean?

CECILIO: Madam, that seems clear enough. Are you going
to ask me to explain what a carnal sin is?

ESTELA: Yes, that's what I want to know. We actresses often
repeat things we don't understand, and when we do, the
critics say we gave a magnificent performance. (*Stares at
the blank.*) Just what is implied by "carnal sin"?

DANIEL: Come, come, Estela! Do you think it's proper to
ask an angel to give you a demonstration?

(Cecilio jumps up and snatches the blanks from each of them.)

CECILIO: I guess I'd better have an oral examination. It will be quicker. I'll question you alone and individually. First you, madam. Will the rest of you go into the dining room till I call you.

DANIEL *(getting up)* :   This method doesn't seem very ethical. But I suppose we are in no position to question the way you proceed. *(At the door of the dining room, he stops.)* Don't you do anything to Estela. Don't touch a hair of her head or you'll account to me for it.

ESTELA *(charmed)* :   Darling, I didn't realize you loved me like that after so many years of marriage.

DANIEL: Don't decide to disintegrate her while I'm in here.

ESTELA: And what made you think I'd let him disintegrate me. Huh! That would be the last straw!

GEORGE: Anyway, behave yourself, Mother. Try not to lie, even though you may find that difficult.

ESTELA *(with dignity)* :   It has never been my habit to lie. Truth is my motto.

GEORGE: A fragile motto, if we're to be frank.

(Exit Daniel, followed by George and Marisol. They close the door behind them. An uncomfortable pause. Cecilio does not know how to start. Finally Estela puts herself into the role of a model hostess.)

ESTELA: Won't you have a cigaret, Ceci. *(Extends a box toward him.)* I always find a cigaret helps, don't you?

CECILIO: We're not permitted to smoke during working hours, madam.

ESTELA: I see. But that's not right, is it? *(in a confidential tone)* Are they very strict up there?

CECILIO: Not very. I'd venture to say, much less than down here. I've seen some of those inspectors you call Internal Revenue that frightened me . . .

ESTELA: That's not strange. It's the same with us.

(*Another uncomfortable pause, during which Cecilio begins to walk back and forth, holding the blanks. Finally he speaks.*)

CECILIO: I've not had much experience in questioning people, you understand. (*He smiles.*) This is my first job like this.

ESTELA (*returning the smile, and in an understanding tone*) :   I understand. You must feel the way I did the first time I stepped onto the stage. It was horrible. My legs trembled. My mouth was dry, and I was sure I'd collapse. Of course I was very young at the time.

CECILIO: You were?

ESTELA: I was barely eighteen. (*a dreamy smile*) And full of ambition to become a star. I was living with a friend at the time, in a tiny apartment. She and I talked night after night about our ambitions. I told her: "There are two ways of becoming a star, Matilde: one to sleep with the director . . ."

CECILIO (*astonished*) :   Oh!

ESTELA: Don't worry. I didn't do that.

CECILIO (*sighing with relief*) :   I'm glad of that. I was afraid I'd have to put down a black mark for you.

ESTELA (*without listening to him*) :   I didn't do it. The director had no interest in sleeping with young actresses. Say what you will, that's just a Chinese tale. There's no easy road to success.

CECILIO: Pardon? Easy road?

ESTELA: Oh, you know what I mean. Don't act stupid!

CECILIO: No, madam. Excuse me, but really I don't know. Up there we always walk on clouds, and therefore every road is easy.

ESTELA: How enchantingly innocent the angels are! But I wasn't referring to that.

CECILIO: No?

ESTELA: No, but I'm perverting you. I'm perverting an angel! I feel like an elderly satyr chasing a nymph. (*She laughs gaily.*)

CECILIO (*seriously*) : Madam, let me remind you that we are examining your life.

ESTELA (*choking off her laughter*): Why do you remind me? I'd almost been able to drive it out of my mind. See, now I'm depressed again.

CECILIO: I'm so sorry! Even though I'm glad you didn't follow the "easy road," whatever that may be; anyway, there's a hundred points in your favor.

ESTELA: Oh, no, I've never had a very sensual temperament. That's the condition of most mortals. It's lack of desire rather than excess of conscience that keeps us from sinning. I prefer the other system for getting ahead.

CECILIO: What other system?

ESTELA (*speaking confidentially*) : Sawing the staircase.

CECILIO: I beg you, madam, to explain what you mean.

ESTELA: Why, everybody knows that's the infallible way. But I'll explain so you'll understand better. And also because some day it may come in handy. I was understudy for the leading lady at the Teatro de la Comedia. She was a fat, unbearable woman, the mistress of the impresario, naturally. And she never got ill. She was as healthy as an animal. If she'd ever got sick, I could have substituted for her. I had my heart on the role, so that's when I sawed the staircase.

CECILIO: What staircase?

ESTELA (*calmly*) : The one to her dressing room. Poor fat old woman! She came tumbling down like a sack of wheat. Naturally she had to spend three weeks in the hospital, and they gave me the chance to play Laura in *Love's Revenge*. That was my first big role, my first great opportunity. From that day on, I never lacked offers. It was so easy: a saw, a staircase, and a bit of determination. (*She smiles with satisfaction.*)

(*Cecilio looks at her for a moment horrified.*)

CECILIO: Don't you realize that was an attempt to murder?

ESTELA (*smiling*): How foolish! Why, the fat old woman was only slightly bruised. I went the next day to the hospital with a box of candy, to see her. She was so happy to see me. It's true that the investigation at the theatre was a bit disagreeable. But it was finally decided that the wood of the stairs was rotten and rats had done the rest. So whenever I give an interview, I usually tell the reporter that I owe my dramatic career to rats.

CECILIO: But you might have killed the actress!

ESTELA: Impossible! She was too fat. Her flesh cushioned her fall.

(*Cecilio stands astonished. He stares at Estela for a speechless moment, then shakes his head.*)

CECILIO: Thank you, madam. That's enough. If you go on remembering incidents, the place below will be too small.

ESTELA: So you've finished examining me?

CECILIO: Yes, yes. I've finished.

ESTELA (*getting up nervously*): What grade do I get, professor? Where will you send me?

CECILIO (*sitting at the table*): I have nothing to do with the grading, madam. That's the job of the Grading Department.

ESTELA: Who's in the Grading Department?

CECILIO: That's a secret. It is changed every year.

ESTELA: Secret? I protest. That's not democratic.

CECILIO: I'm sorry, but all I do is fill in the forms and return them. You may go now, madam. (*Starts writing.*) And please send in your husband.

ESTELA: Daniel? I'm afraid he won't have much to report. He's the most boring person in the world. (*She approaches Cecilio at the table.*) If you want to know how many times he's been unfaithful to me, I can tell you about that better than he can. (*fingering one hand*) Let me see. Yes, I think the first time was with Tere. She was my intimate friend. She bleaches her hair and she is very passionate.

CECILIO (*interrupting her*):   Madam, my instructions are to interview the people concerned, and personally. So please ask him to come in.

ESTELA (*shrugging*):   Very well. Any way you like. But you'll find it terribly boring. (*She turns.*) Don't forget I warned you.

(*She goes toward the dining room. Cecilio continues writing. In a moment, enter Daniel. He is evidently hesitant. He stops just inside the room, as if waiting for orders.*)

CECILIO: Don't be afraid. Nothing will happen to you. Really I can't understand the fear of all of you mortals facing a situation that was bound to come sooner or later.

DANIEL: I'd prefer it later than sooner, Mr. Angel. That's the way we all feel.

CECILIO: Death is the only sure thing in the world.

DANIEL: That's true, very true. Sure and entirely unknown. That's the trouble. If anyone had ever come back from the other world and had told us about it, we'd feel easier about it all.

CECILIO (*warningly*):   The whole thing is to reach the other world, as you call it, with an easy conscience. Don't you think so?

DANIEL (*without conviction*):   Oh, yes. Certainly. That's just what the Church keeps telling us.

CECILIO: That's the purpose of this examination. It's a sort of cleansing. He offers to unburden your consciences. In short, to wipe them clean, as clean as an unborn baby.

DANIEL: Just! Extremely just!

CECILIO: Very well, then. Now let's see.

(Before he can continue and at the moment that Cecilio picks up one of the blanks, Daniel begins talking in a flood of rapid words.)

DANIEL: I'm afraid in my case you won't have much to put down, Mr. Angel. I mean in my case everything is as clean as the sky in springtime. You'll see, Mr. Angel. *(a little doubtfully)* Or should I address you as Mr. Examining Angel? You'll have to excuse me if I bungle. You see I never had much experience in celestial protocol. No, I think I'll continue with Mr. Angel. That's easier. I've always been a hard-working man. I owe my present position to the honest work of my hands. *(He holds them out and looks nervously at them.)* Honest, reliable, upright. That's what I've always been. My life might be considered exemplary. An example of a devoted citizen who, in a democracy like ours, has come to occupy a high place in society entirely because of his own efforts and his devotion to work, to honorable, upright, blameless work.

(His long speech has left him breathless. He wipes his forehead with his handkerchief.)

CECILIO *(astonished)*:   Why, you're quite an orator, my esteemed Mr. González. I'd advise you up there to seek a seat in Parliament.

DANIEL *(anxiously)*:   Thank you, thank you. So you think they may send me up there?

CECILIO: That's hard to say till I know more about your life.

DANIEL: Why, I've told you my whole life, an honest, upright, industrious life.

CECILIO: Yes, yes. I heard all that. But don't you remember anything that blemished so exemplary a life?

DANIEL *(shaking his head vigorously)* :   No! No, absolutely nothing.

CECILIO *(insistant)* :   No blemish, no stains, no slips?

DANIEL: No, indeed. Maybe a few sentimental pecadillos. A couple of amorous adventures, perhaps.

CECILIO: That's not the sort of blemish I mean, Mr. González. Those are stains that can easily be removed in His eyes. I mean things of greater moral importance.

DANIEL: Nothing!

CECILIO *(looking at him fixedly)* :   Nothing?

(Daniel shakes his head vigorously.)

CECILIO: You're sure?

(Again Daniel denies everything.)

CECILIO: Very well, my esteemed Mr. González. A conscious and persistent falsehood is a hundred points against you.

DANIEL: Conscious falsehood?

CECILIO: What you're affirming right now is a conscious lie. *(A pause. Cecilio confronts him.)* What have you forgotten to tell me about some shares in The Unlucky Mine?

DANIEL *(confused)* :   The Unlucky Mine?

CECILIO: Exactly. It's an unlucky coincidence that the matter of the ownership of stock in the Unlucky Mine should be brought to your attention just at this time. You falsified the stock, didn't you?

DANIEL: How did you know?

CECILIO *(stepping back)* :   So you finally confess it! I know everything. We up there know everything.

DANIEL: I should have realized that! But that happened thirty years ago, Mr. Angel, and I was the only one in the office when it happened.

CECILIO: That's where you are wrong. Time is merely an illusion that you mortals invented. For us up there, it doesn't exist. You might have falsified the stock a minute ago. And as for being the only one in the office, you're wrong again. I was sitting on your file cabinet. Of course at that time I was invisible. I remember the occasion clearly. It was when He sent me the first time to check government auditors. They were committing frauds in public affairs, as usual. I even visited the Ministries. A never-ending story! Alas for those who get involved with fiscal employees! It can get pretty tricky.

DANIEL: I confess that I falsified the stock, but without evil intent, and I made everything good. Anyway, when I confess it, I get forgiven, don't I?

CECILIO: Yes, after a free confession. But it seems to me a great many people might have been hurt by that falsification that became the foundation of your later fortune. Am I right?

DANIEL (*stammering*): As far as being the foundation . . . Well, I'll admit it was helpful, but you'd hardly call it the foundation.

CECILIO: Very well. I think we can consider the examination concluded. You may leave, Mr. González.

DANIEL (*anxiously*): But what about the decision? What's the verdict?

CECILIO: As I told your wife, I'm merely the examiner. All I do is fill in the questionnaire. Grading it is the work of the Grading Department. You will learn the results tomorrow.

DANIEL: But . . . but before then, is it possible to learn anything?

CECILIO: Quite impossible, sir!

DANIEL: Not even if I should grease the machine with a blank check?

CECILIO (*angrily*): Mr. González, do you realize what

you're proposing? It's nothing less than bribery. You're trying to bribe me.

DANIEL: Don't take offense, Mr. Angel. That's the way it is usually done with employees on earth. It's the customary way of speeding a transaction. We call it "Oiling the wheels."

CECILIO: Well! It's not customary among us, sir.

DANIEL: Excuse me, then, I assure you, Mr. Angel, that I had no intention of offending you.

CECILIO: You're excused, Mr. González. Now be good enough to send your son in.

DANIEL (*backing toward the door*): Yes, yes. Just as you say.

(*He hurries out. Cecilio shakes his head and smiles.*)

CECILIO: These people down here! They think they can smooth out anything with money. As if money was good for anything up there!

(*Enter George.*)

GEORGE (*airily*): Well, I guess the hour of final judgment has come.

CECILIO: It has for you, young man.

GEORGE: Listen. At the University we have a final judgment from December to January, when they hold exams. So we get hardened to examinations. What's one more, or one less? (*Makes a scornful gesture.*)

CECILIO: I'm glad you feel that way about it, Most mortals have a dread of it.

GEORGE: Nonsense! For us, the young people of today, that whole yarn about a Final Judgment is nothing but another device of those "up there." One more farce, that's all.

CECILIO: I beg you, young man, to show more respect. But what do you mean by "device"?

GEORGE: A political scheme by those "up there" to give their bureaucrats something to keep busy about. Just like government business on earth.

CECILIO: I didn't bring you here to talk politics with you.

GEORGE: That's where you are wrong, Mr. Exterminating Angel. As long as you're in Chile, you'll have to talk politics. It's the national pastime. Everybody in Chile indulges in it.

CECILIO: That's why they're the way they are. Even "up there," we hear talk of the Chilean maladies.

GEORGE: The Chilean maladies, plural? (*He laughs loudly.*) But if we talked about just one malady—though I wouldn't call it by such a name. It's more a vice.

CECILIO: What is it?

GEORGE: Just what I said. Politics. (*He approaches Cecilio confidentially.*) Listen. You're mistaken. There are only a few sinners down here for you to judge: the politicians.

CECILIO: Really?

GEORGE: Absolutely, my dear Angel. If you start making an inventory of political sins, you'd have to fill a pile of blanks from here up to there.

CECILIO: Do you mean there are no good politicians on this asteroid?

GEORGE (*casually*): Oh, yes . . . The dead ones.

CECILIO: That's enough, young man. I warn you that slander of your fellowmen is a major sin. And if you keep on with it, that will make it very hard for you to pass the examination.

GEORGE: Bah! You're just like all the other professors. I thought those up there would be smarter. "Pass the exam! Pass the exam!" Why, passing an exam is the easiest thing in the world.

CECILIO: Yes, for those who study.

GEORGE: Study? How square can you get? Why, nobody in Chile studies, man! Life is short and we've got to enjoy

every minute of it. Who knows where we'll be tomorrow?

CECILIO (*thoughtfully*) :   Very true. Who knows where?

GEORGE: Bah! But I'd forgotten. You ought to know. Tell
me, Mr. Examining Angel, is it terribly boring in the
place where they're intending to send me? What are the
girls like? Worth a second glance?

CECILIO: They're of all kinds, just like down here. (*suddenly serious*) But let's have a little respect, you beard-
less cynic! In a moment we're starting an examination
of your life, and this is the Day of Judgment.

GEORGE: So what? It's just like any other day. I don't see
any difference.

CECILIO (*annoyed*) :   Very well, but you don't need to
sound so tough. You make me nervous.

GEORGE (*contrite*) :   Excuse me, Mr. Angel. I'll promise seriousness from now on. I know you're only doing your
job. How much do they pay you "up there"?

CECILIO: Very little. Our salaries are very low.

GEORGE: Then let me give you a tip. Complain to the
Department of Labor.

CECILIO (*confidentially*) :   That's just what I'm planning to
do as soon as I get back. (*serious again*) Enough! Now
have you anything to confess? Any major sins?

GEORGE (*in joking tones*) :   I'm guilty, Father, guilty. I copied the final examinations for graduation from beginning to end. How about that? Is that serious enough for
you? (*He smiles with satisfaction.*)

CECILIO (*writing in the blank*) :   Anything else?

GEORGE: Isn't that enough?

CECILIO (*implacably*) :   Anything else?

GEORGE: You want a lot. Let's see. All I can remember are a
few minor sins. A cute girl here, another there, but of
course I've always been careful. Never any conse-
quences.

CECILIO (*getting to his feet*) :   That sort of sin isn't in my department. You may leave. Send in your sister, please.

GEORGE: Marisol? (*He goes toward the door.*) You aren't kidding? What do you expect that youngster to confess? Why, she hasn't harmed a fly. She tries to make out she's a dangerous woman, a femme fatale, but when it comes time to make something out of it, she's chicken.

CECILIO: Never mind! Send her in.

GEORGE (*with an exaggerated bow*): As you request, Mr. Angel. You're the boss. You're in charge. (*As he is about to open the door, he stops.*) Hey, tell me, what you got planned for tonight?

CECILIO: What?

GEORGE: Never mind. I was going to invite you to a game of poker with the gang and afterward we could take a whirl and meet some of my friends. There's one blonde! (*Gestures feminine curves.*) I'll tell the world, some blonde.

CECILIO (*sternly*): I told you. Send in your sister.

GEORGE: O.K., my dear Angel, O.K. Don't get mad! I thought you might go for blondes. But if they're not your dish, forget it, and we can still be friends.

(*Exit George. Cecilio shakes his head in disgust. Enter Marisol. Her attitude is a challenge, a challenge with feminine weapons.*)

MARISOL: Here I am. (*She stops at the door.*)

CECILIO: Won't you please come in?

(*She enters slowly, hips swaying, but not saying a word. Pause.*)

MARISOL: Well, I suppose you're very proud of yourself, aren't you? Sneak into a house of honorable people, pass yourself off as a servant, and then turn out to be . . . Well, I don't want even to think about it.

CECILIO: I had my orders.

MARISOL: I've come into contact with all sorts of men during my long and adventurous existence, but with a fellow like you, never! And to think you call yourself an angel!

CECILIO: Permit me to remind you that this is the Day of Judgment and talk like that may get you into trouble.

MARISOL: And now the insolent fellow is trying to frighten me. We'll see about that.

CECILIO: Will you keep still! (*He picks up a blank.*)

MARISOL: Otherwise you'll disintegrate me, no doubt.

CECILIO: Exactly! (*Reads the blank.*) Remember this is a matter of . . .

MARISOL (*casually lighting a cigaret*): Yes, I know what it is a matter of. You don't have to give me a sermon. You've said enough times that this is the Day of the Last Judgment.

CECILIO: Remember it, then.

MARISOL: And I'm expected to confess my sins.

CECILIO: Exactly!

MARISOL (*in a firm voice*): Very well. I'll confess the only thing that makes men interested in a girl of my age. (*in a natural tone*) I'm a virgin.

CECILIO (*scandalized*): Señorita! I did not ask you anything like that.

MARISOL: But you were thinking it. I could see it in your face. You were speculating: "Is she or isn't she?"

CECILIO: You saw nothing in my face. We angels never reveal in our faces what we are thinking about. That's one great advantage of being an angel. Haven't you ever heard the expression "an angelic expression"?

MARISOL: I suppose that's the result of some new make-up. But that doesn't convince me. Anyway, write it down so you may have it in black and white. I'm a virgin. Write it in big letters, please, and show it to those up there for whatever use they may want to make of it. It'll shake them up. Nowadays it's not easy to find a virgin on earth.

CECILIO: That's true. Yet they say there were once eleven thousand martyred at one time.

MARISOL: That's just a tradition. But write down about me, please.

CECILIO (*busily writing*): And if it's . . . if it's true what you say, why do you adopt this air of a femme fatale?

MARISOL: Because men go for it. At least they do down here. They detest virgins. What do you think would happen if a girl like me, eighteen years old, nearly, went around proclaiming right and left that she was still a virgin?

CECILIO: I haven't the slightest idea.

MARISOL: Quite obviously you don't know the world, my dear angel. Being a professional angel, you always live in the clouds. If a girl like me didn't seem like a vampire, she'd never interest a man. If they know she's a virgin, they avoid her like the plague. Men of my generation are fascinated by second-hand women.

CECILIO: That's a strange preference.

(*Marisol approaches him insinuatingly.*)

MARISOL: My poor, dear angel, how many things I could teach you, things an angel never once suspected.

CECILIO (*with an appreciative glance*): I'm sure you could teach me a lot. (*tentatively*) Yes, a great deal. (*Pulls himself together.*) But . . . no! Rules, paragraph five, section three.

MARISOL: Let's forget section three, shall we?

CECILIO: I'm tempted. (*raising his eyes to heaven*) Lord, why do You set me in the midst of such temptations?

MARISOL: What are you saying, Angel dear?

CECILIO (*continuing his thoughts*): To tempt me, no doubt. To strengthen me. And I shall be worthy of my mission. I'll dodge all temptations, even the most fascinating ones. (*He draws back.*) Señorita, shall we get on with the examination? (*He takes up the blank and considers it.*)

MARISOL (*disillusioned*): That man must be an iceberg. No man ever resisted me like him. They're right that angels aren't flesh and blood. (*with a sudden idea*) Or did the fact that I'm a virgin scare you off?

CECILIO: Señorita, I'm asking the questions here, not you? Have you any major sin to confess?

MARISOL: O.K., back to the sins. Major, what you might call big, fat sins, no. But one that may be a sin, depending on how you look at it . . .

CECILIO: Please explain.

MARISOL (*calmly*): I "lifted" Nené Guzmán's fiancé.

CECILIO: What do you mean, lifted? Does that mean you picked him up?

MARISOL (*laughing*): No, silly. I lifted him because he transferred his affections from Nené to me, and he stood her up, left her planted.

CECILIO: Planted? Like a tree?

MARISOL: More or less. Do you understand?

CECILIO: Yes, I understand. You mean you stole him away from her.

MARISOL: Don't think it was because I liked him. I did it as a test. Everybody says I have a touch and calls me "Sticky fingers," and I just wanted to see whether I deserved the reputation.

CECILIO: Seems to me that's an evil thing to do.

MARISOL: Why, I thought it was a good deed, and I expected you, dear angel, to give me good marks for it.

CECILIO: A good deed? To take a friend's sweetheart away from her?

MARISOL: I didn't say she was exactly a friend of mine. But I'll tell you how it turned out. Nené was heart broken. She cried all day and got thinner and thinner. Then her parents decided to take her away from Chile and all memories of that ungrateful sweetheart. So they took her on a trip around the world. You see, I really did her a good turn.

CECILIO: But your intentions were evil.

MARISOL: If the road to Hell is paved with good intentions, as they say, it stands to reason the road to Heaven is paved with evil intentions. Because if I hadn't lifted Claudio, Nené would never have got to Paris. I often tell her she's indebted to me for her trip to Europe, but she still doesn't give me credit for that.

CECILIO: Well, that's one way of looking at it, but I'm afraid those up there won't take that point of view.

(*The door opens. Enter Estela, followed by Daniel and George.*)

ESTELA: For heaven's sake, Ceci, why all this delay in the examination? You've got us all with our nerves on edge. After all, we're a model family, unlike most others. Why we have hardly any sins. Imagine what hundreds of others are confessing! Tons of infractions.

GEORGE: What wouldn't you give, Mother, to overhear some of them?

DANIEL: What Estela means, Cecilio, is to ask whether you can't make an exception in our case.

CECILIO (*puzzled*):   Exception?

ESTELA: Yes, we've been discussing it. Look, Ceci, since we're a model family—and you can't deny that—why not leave us as the only survivors on earth after all the rest have disappeared?

CECILIO: But, madam . . .

ESTELA (*laughing*):   Imagine the expression on Saruca Aguirre's face! She'll be green with envy in Limbo, or wherever she is.

DANIEL: Come on, Cecilio. Grant my wife what she wants.

GEORGE: You might as well give in when Mother wants something. She always gets what she wants. Once she takes an idea into her head, she's quite capable of going to Heaven itself and arguing with St. Peter.

(Suddenly Cecilio stiffens. His voice sounds strange.)

CECILIO: Silence! Everybody, silence!

(All stand astonished, expectant, watching with curiosity. Cecilio gives the impression that he is hearing voices inaudible to the others. His attitude is of intense concentration.)

CECILIO: Yes, Lord! Right away, Lord!

(He hurries to the radio and turns it on. The others group around him.)

RADIO: All over the world, the Day of Last Judgment continues with no serious incidents occurring. In Rome the head of the Communist Party declared that the Last Judgment was only a farce invented by capitalists to expand their imperialistic economic policy of exploiting the masses. In Cairo, . . .

(Suddenly the broadcast is interrupted and the impressive thunderclaps of the first act are repeated.)

ESTELA *(with a sudden shriek)* :   Good heavens!

DANIEL: It's just a sudden storm in the Andes, dear.

CECILIO: Silence! Silence! *(He listens attentively to the thunder.)* Yes, Lord, I'm here. Exterminating Angel XM 26. *(more thunder)* What's that? Why, that's impossible, Boss! But the blanks are already filled out. No, Lord, that can't be done. *(imperious thunder)* Yes, Lord. Yes, I know You're the one who gives the orders. But that will completely alter our plans. Don't You realize that these mortals are already reconciled to going to Heaven, Limbo, or—the other place? *(more intense thunder)* Very well, Boss. Your will be done. But what are we going to do about all these people on earth? (*thunder*) Yes, Master, yes. I'll carry out everything as You command. (*The thunder ceases and beautiful music is heard of the sort that might be described as heavenly.*)

ESTELA (*timidly*) : That . . . ? Was that really He?

CECILIO: Yes, madam.

ESTELA: He has a striking voice. I like it. If he cleared up his diction a bit, He would be a success in the theatre.

DANIEL: Estela, please! . . . Cecilio, tell us what is happening?

CECILIO (*going to the door in bad humor*) : Everything has been changed. It's all upside-down. What a time to have some new whim!

(*Before their astonished eyes, he walks out.*)

MARISOL: What did all that mean?

ESTELA: Probably the one up there has agreed to our request. We'll be the only family left on earth when the Last Judgment is over. We shall be famous, the most virtuous family of the universe.

DANIEL: Didn't sound like that to me. Those thunder claps were pretty loud.

GEORGE: Yes, they sounded angry.

(*Marisol runs to take refuge in her mother's arms.*)

MARISOL: Mother, I'm scared.

ESTELAS Don't be silly, daughter. If he sends us down to H_____ I mean to the other place, you can use that red Dior dress that we paid so much for. It will harmonize marvelously with your surroundings.

(*As all stare, limp and worried*)

THE CURTAIN FALLS

ACT **3**

A half hour has passed. The characters are in the same condition, now sitting and staring at the door through which Cecilio disappeared. With their heads in their hands, they look depressed. The radio is still playing soft, almost celestial music. There is a silence.

ESTELA: They've been playing that music for half an hour.

DANIEL: What do you think is happening out there? The news flash said they would be issuing bulletins every ten minutes, but we haven't heard a thing.

GEORGE: Maybe the announcer has been carried off to . . . you know where. (*He laughs, but none of the others join him.*)

MARISOL: Only someone like you with your bad taste would be making jokes at a moment like this.

GEORGE: Well, it's better than sitting around as though attending a funeral, when so far we've had nothing but the prelude.

MARISOL (*jumping up hysterically*):   Mother, if George goes on talking like that, I think I'll scream at the top of my voice.

GEORGE: Go ahead, Sis. It'll make you feel better.

ESTELA: Don't tease her, Georgie.

GEORGE: All I said was a general remark. I wasn't talking about her. But she, that lovely girl who gets all her beauty out of a bottle, thinks everything said refers to her fascinating personality.

DANIEL: Stop it, children! Can't you stop fighting on the Day of Last Judgment?

MARISOL (*sitting down*):   It's habit, Daddy.

DANIEL: What I wonder is, what's happening to Cecilio. He walked out of here more than a half hour ago.

ESTELA: Leaving us all upset, without any explanation. How inconsiderate!

GEORGE: Maybe he's made a quick trip up there. (*gesturing*

with a finger) Perhaps for some urgent conference. He
seemed very worried.

MARISOL: George, turn off the radio. I can't stand that
music. It gets on my nerves.

ESTELA: Yes, Georgie, turn off the radio. It's quite obvious
that something terrible has happened to that good-for-
nothing announcer and he isn't going to talk any more.

(*George gets up and turns off the radio. Then he sits
down again with a depressed air. Another long period
of silence.*)

ESTELA (*suddenly and almost screaming*) :   Daniel!

DANIEL: What's the matter, woman?

ESTELA: You've got to go right out there and see what Ceci
is doing. (*after a pause*) We've waited for him long
enough.

DANIEL (*not very enthusiastic*) :   Me?

ESTELA: Yes . . . you.

DANIEL: Why not George? He's younger and more agile. I
mean if agility should be needed.

ESTELA: You're the head of the family, Daniel. It's your
duty to go. In all the plays, it's always the head of the
family that undertakes the dangerous missions.

MARISOL: Yes, Daddy, you must go. I can't stand any more
of this.

DANIEL (*dubiously*) :   But suppose he disintegrates me?

ESTELA: Don't talk nonsense! He's only an angel of the
third category. How could he disintegrate you?

GEORGE: Are you afraid, Father?

DANIEL (*getting up slowly*) :   Afraid? Me? Don't be foolish.
(*Starts toward the door.*) I'll find out what is happening to Cecilio.

(*Estela jumps up and hands him a big vase.*)

ESTELA: Here. Take this for a weapon. It may be of some
use.

(Daniel takes the vase and starts out with a heroic stride.)

DANIEL: If anything happens to me, my dear family, we'll meet again up there. *(Exit Daniel.)*

GEORGE: Poor Father. He's scared to death.

ESTELA: Have more respect for your father. He's never been afraid. He's one of the bravest men I know. That's why he married me.

MARISOL: But what can have happened? I'm going crazy! They are going to send us all down to Hell.

ESTELA: Oh, Marisol. Don't use that word.

(Marisol begins to pace nervously.)

MARISOL: Don't you realize? This is the Last Judgment. The calmness of all of you amazes me. An angel has written down all our sins, one after another without omitting any. We're just about to confront the Supreme Judge. And at the very instant that angel was going to tell us the result, what happened? The angel talked with his boss, and paff! he disappeared. Doesn't that strike you as strange? To me, it's terrifying. It's a bad omen.

ESTELA: Maybe it isn't.

MARISOL: Mother, you're always full of rosy illusions.

ESTELA *(getting up)*: Marisol, do you think that . . . ? *(making a despairing gesture)*

MARISOL: That's just what I've been thinking. He got orders to exterminate us all instantly, and he's out there making plans. That must be what the thunder meant. We have been condemned.

GEORGE: What a morbid imagination, Sister.

ESTELA *(terrified)*: My God! My poor Daniel has gone in there! *(gesturing toward the door where Cecilio disappeared)* I'll never see him again. He's already disintegrated.

(The door opens. Enter Daniel, calm and smiling. Estela hurls herself upon him and embraces him in a frenzy.)

ESTELA: Daniel! My dear Daniel!

DANIEL: Easy, wife, easy! Nothing has happened to me.

MARISOL *(anxiously)* :   Have you seen him, Daddy?

DANIEL: Not actually. He was locked in his room. But I talked to him through the door. A very entertaining conversation.

ESTELA *(with a tragic gesture)* :   He uttered our sentence of death! I knew it.

DANIEL: Not at all. He merely asked me to be patient for a few minutes and then he'd come out here and give us all some very important news.

GEORGE: What kind of news?

DANIEL: He wouldn't tell me. All he said was he wanted us all to remain together.

ESTELA: Mass disintegration! Probably with an atomic bomb.

(Enter Cecilio, dressed as on his arrival. He carries a small valise and a hat in one hand, and the blanks in the other. Those on stage, too worried about their own problems, do not notice him until he speaks.)

CECILIO *(in gentle tones)* :   Your attention, if you please.

(All turn toward him, with cries of fright.)

ESTELA: For Heaven's sake, Ceci, don't do that again! You almost frightened me to death.

CECILIO: Don't do what, madam?

ESTELA: Come in like that without making a sound.

MARISOL: Yes, you sneak in like a thief *(doubtfully)* or an executioner.

CECILIO: I assure you, señorita, I'm neither.

DANIEL: Yes, we know who you are, nevertheless we don't have any nerves left. This waiting is killing us.

GEORGE: Father, don't keep repeating that.

CECILIO *(calmly)* :   Then you'll be glad to know the waiting is over.

(He gives each one his own questionnaire.)

ESTELA *(looking at hers)* :   What's the meaning of this? What are we supposed to do with these papers?

MARISOL: I hope this isn't another of your jokes. If it is, I don't see anything funny.

CECILIO: It's no joke, señorita. Those questionnaires are yours from now on.

ESTELA: What do you want us to do with them?

CECILIO: Oh, I don't care. That's not in my department. However I'd suggest you study them. It isn't every day that a person gets the opportunity of reading an X-ray of his life. Think of the saving in psychiatric expense.

ESTELA: I've never gone to a psychiatrist.

MARISOL: Do you consider us clinical cases, Ce? Do you think we are in need of psychiatry and all that trap?

CECILIO: It's not my duty to decide, señorita. At any rate, I can't take these questionnaires with me. They weigh too much. As they say on the airlines, "excess baggage."

DANIEL: You can't take them with you? Do you mean, Cecilio, that you are going away?

CECILIO: Exactly, sir.

ESTELA: Oh, no. I protest! I protest vigorously. On the Day of the Last Judgment, you can't leave us all alone and unprotected. No, indeed!

CECILIO *(slowly)* :   There won't be a Last Judgment. It has been postponed.

ALL *(in unison)* :   What?

CECILIO: For the present, there won't be a Last Judgment. Those are the orders I received a while ago. You yourselves heard them over the radio.

ESTELA: We heard thunder, but we didn't understand anything.

MARISOL: Do you mean we're not going to be judged?

CECILIO: That's true, señorita.

GEORGE: Do you mean filling out those questionnaires and practically making public confessions was wasted time?

CECILIO: You must understand, sir . . . Change of plans up there.

ESTELA *(furiously)* :   I call that cruelty. Yes, it's worse. It's abuse of confidence. I confessed to you some horrible things, things I wouldn't even tell my pillow. If any reporters got ahold of them, they'd spread the scandal across every rag in the capital and that would be the end of my career.

CECILIO: But, madam . . .

ESTELA: No "buts." You just go ahead with this Last Judgment. After practically stripping me naked in public, the least that can be done is carry it through. That's what we women always demand under such circumstances. *(Approaches Cecilio menacingly.)* No, indeed, Ceci! Whether you want it or not, you've got to go on with your boasted Last Judgment.

MARISOL: Mother is right.

DANIEL: Yes, for once, she's right.

GEORGE: Absolutely.

CECILIO: Hmm, that's all very fine, but you mortals seem to have forgotten one important detail: He is the one who determines destiny. He does it any way He wants, and nobody can discuss it, certainly not mortals. You should be happy that He is giving you the privilege of living for a while longer.

ESTELA: Then what did all that thunder mean?

CECILIO: It was an order for the immediate suspension of plans for a Last Judgment, a peremptory order that allows no argument.

(He goes to the sofa and puts down his valise and hat.)

ESTELA *(sitting down)* :   Well, if the Last Judgment has

been postponed, that means we're innocent and don't deserve any such catastrophe.

CECILIO: You're quite wrong, madam. His reasons are just the opposite.

ESTELA: All right, Ceci. What are they?

CECILIO (*slowly*) : It's not for me to use words that wound, madam. All I'll say is that He thinks a Last Judgment would be very dangerous at this time.

ESTELA: Dangerous? I suppose you mean we'd all be in danger of being exterminated. How foolish!

CECILIO: Not dangerous for you, madam. For those up there.

MARISOL: What do you mean?

CECILIO: That's what He believes, and I might add that it's not His opinion alone. As is done in all good democracies, He consulted with the Parliament of Higher Angels. They are of the same opinion.

GEORGE: Parliament of Higher Angels? So they have politics up there? Bravo! That'll be my career when I get there.

CECILIO: And it's just on account of young people like you, if you'll allow me, sir, that He thinks it would be unwise for the human race in its present state to be allowed up there, yet.

ESTELA: But you can't accuse me of youth. That's not one of my sins.

CECILIO: Without intention of offending you, madam, your thoughtlessness could completely disorganize celestial order.

ESTELA: That's the limit! To call me thoughtless when all my life I've been an example of professional and private thoughtfulness. How unjust! (*with a dramatic gesture*)

CECILIO (*to Marisol*) : As for you, señorita, He believes you are a typical example of what they call "the angry young generation."

MARISOL: Angry? Me? I protest. That's an insult.

CECILIO: And thousands of others girls like you would arrive up there if the Last Judgment took place now,
charming girls, pleasant, bubbling with vitality, but
without morals or principles. A lot of coquettes.

MARISOL   (*approaching Cecilio insinuatingly*) :   Do you
think I'm charming and coquettish, Ce? Tell me.

CECILIO   (*fleeing from her*) :   Much too much so, señorita.
And I'm afraid many of my companions up there would
have the same opinion.

MARISOL: How fascinating. To seduce millions of angels.
Something I've always dreamed of.

CECILIO: He thinks that if even two exponents of the
younger generation like you (*nodding to Marisol and
George*) should filter in up there, it would cause all
sorts of complications. Our rhythm of life is different,
slow, easy-going. But you with your high speed autos,
your television, your devilish music, oh, no!

DANIEL: But nobody could object to me, Cecilio.

CECILIO: Oh, you, sir! He believes that if you took it on
yourself to reorganize the economy up there, it would
be much improved, but at the same time its moral tone
would be greatly lowered, if you understand.

DANIEL: I'm afraid I do.

ESTELA: In other words, those up there are afraid of us.

MARISOL: Mother!

ESTELA: Might as well call things by their right names,
dear. (*dropping her voice*) at least now that we've
apparently escaped the Last Judgment.

CECILIO: You are frightening, esteemed madam. You hu-
mans possess power for corruption for which we up
there aren't ready. (*pointing to George*) The political
principles of the young people of today; (*pointing to
Marisol*) the moral tendencies—or should I say immoral?—of the modern generation; (*to Estela*) the enchanting thoughtlessness of mature people; (*to Daniel*) the lack of scruples of today's business men. No,

that's too much. We're not capable of coping with them under present conditions. So we'll wait till the human race matures.

MARISOL *(with a burst of laughter)* : So Heaven isn't prepared to receive mortals! That's funny. We were so frightened about the Last Judgment, and now it turns out that they up there were the really frightened ones.

(Cecilio begins to pick up his possessions.)

ESTELA *(following him)* : But Ceci, do you think they would have sent us up there? Suppose they had planned to send us to the other place. *(Gestures downward.)*

CECILIO: What?

MARISOL: What if we'd been doomed to Hell?

CECILIO: Señorita, please don't name it in my presence.

GEORGE: But one can't rule out the possibility of a trip to that region.

CECILIO: The other place is in a bad situation these days. Since the recent reforms in the Church, the chief down there is very pessimistic. He doesn't believe he can handle anybody until his kingdom is completely reorganized.

ESTELA: What a pity! I'd already begun to think during the Last Judgment of what clothes I might wear, if I go there.

CECILIO: Don't be discouraged, madam. If it's any comfort, I'll tell you what He thinks. He believes that in a few years more you people on earth will be able to organize your own Last Judgment. You possess all the elements.

MARISOL: What do you mean? What about the seven promised thunder-claps mentioned in the Bible?

GEORGE: And the seven golden vials full of the wrath of God?

DANIEL: And the two witnesses who prophecied drought?

ESTELA: And those famous horses and the Four Horsemen of the Apocalypse?

CECILIO: My dear friends, you'll soon be able to provide those for yourselves. A few years ago you devised the most formidable apocalyptic machine ever created in history. Don't give up hope. Even as far off as Peking, they're making their preparations.

MARISOL: A Chinese Last Judgment. How exotic!

ESTELA: I refuse to participate in a Last Judgment organized by the Russians or the Chinese. It wouldn't be spectacular.

MARISOL: Mother is right to a certain degree. To make us feel we had come to the Last Judgment, something more is necessary, even if it's only sinister music played on a church organ.

CECILIO: You mortals are incorrigible. You'll never learn. But some day you'll feel that terror . . . when He considers that the moment has come for the Last Judgment, when things begin to happen.

GEORGE: What things?

CECILIO: That which is written. At that moment, those lives that have no goal, those beings that can't justify their existence, will perish, or simply disappear. And the chosen ones will survive.

DANIEL: But, heavens, that's not the end of the world.

CECILIO: My dear sir, the Last Judgment isn't the end of the world. It's only the end of its infancy and the beginning of its maturity. (*He picks up his valise and hat.*) Now you know everything and my mission down here is ended.

ESTELA (*alarmed*): Ceci, you aren't leaving! At least have a cup of tea first.

CECILIO: If I should stay longer on earth, madam, my visit would have no purpose. There's a lot of bureaucratic work that is waiting for me up there.

MARISOL (*again approaching him*): We've become so accustomed to you, Ce, even if there were a few memorable clashes.

CECILIO (*backing away*) :   All I can do is thank you for your kindness and ask your forgiveness if I caused you any alarm or uncomfortable moments. But you'll understand, I hope. Business is business.

DANIEL: We'll miss you. Cecilio.

CECILIO: Thank you, sir.

GEORGE: We'll all miss you.

ESTELA: It was so nice to have an angel in the house. So chic!

MARISOL: Even if was only an angel of the third category.

CECILIO (*putting on his hat*) :   And now may I go to the roof?

ESTELA: The roof? Good heavens, you aren't thinking of suicide!

CECILIO (*smiling*) :   Don't worry, madam. I need a high place to take off. This way I won't have to climb to the top of San Cristóbal like all the other angels.

ESTELA: Take off? You mean with your own wings?

CECILIO: Of course!

GEORGE: That I want to see, Ceci, a real jet-propelled angel!

CECILIO: May I use the roof?

DANIEL: Oh, no! The roof is too dangerous. Some of the tile are loose. You might slip and fall before you could get airborn.

MARISOL: What about the balcony?

ESTELA: Of course! The balcony. That's a fine idea, Marisol. The whole neighborhood will die of envy when they see an angel flying away from my house.

CECILIO: Very well. I'll use the balcony.

(*George opens wide the double doors to the balcony. It must be opened in such a way that the actual take-off of Cecilio is hidden from the audience, but at the same time they can watch the reactions of the actors as the angel flies away.*)

GEORGE: How about this?

(Cecilio turns to them, visibly moved.)

CECILIO: Well, this is farewell, dear friends. But it need not
be a sad farewell. I'm sure we'll see one another again
up there. I hope not too soon. I know how you mortals
fear the final leap. But believe me, I'll be waiting for
you when the moment arrives.

(Estela embraces him and gives him a noisy kiss.)

ESTELA: Goodbye, Ceci. Pleasant trip. It's a pity you have
to go. *(Gives him another kiss.)* Now I can boast to
Saruca Aguirre that I kissed an angel.

DANIEL *(shaking hands with him)*:   Thanks, Cecilio, especially for the Valderrama affair.

GEORGE: I hope you enjoy yourself up there, Ceci. Tell me
when there are some tough political problems to settle
and I'll take a flier up there and see what I can do.

MARISOL: Remember me once in a while, Ce. Remember a
girl who could easily have learned to love an angel.

CECILIO *(in a melancholy tone)*:   Every day I'll think of
you, too. When you look up into the sky and see the
splendor of the sun on the clouds, you'll know I'm
there. *(He goes out onto the balcony.)*

ESTELA *(dramatically)*:   It makes me want to cry.

DANIEL: Control yourself, Estela. *(They crowd about the
balcony door.)*

ESTELA: What neat wings!

GEORGE: Now let's see how he takes off.

DANIEL: There he goes!

ESTELA *(shouting)*:   Careful, Ceci! Increase your speed!
Straighten your feet.

MARISOL: Watch out for the wind, Ce. Don't fall in the
middle of Santiago.

DANIEL: Ah, there! Now he's safely in flight.

GEORGE: You could hardly hear him. He makes lots less

The Man of the Century

noise than a jet plane. Of course he flies slower. But he's gaining speed now.

ESTELA: He's getting smaller and smaller. Look!

MARISOL: He's no bigger than a canary.

ESTELA: He's only a dot in the sky. A ray of the sun on a cloud, as he said.

(*Silence. They return slowly and drop into chairs without a word.*)

MARISOL: He was nice.

DANIEL: He was a fine fellow . . . for an angel.

ESTELA: And so interested in the theatre. What a leading man he would have made!

GEORGE: If all angels are like him, it won't be so frightening the day we arrive up there. At least we can count on one friend. (*silence*)

ESTELA (*slowly*): Georgie . . .

GEORGE: Yes, Mother?

ESTELA: You'll have to put another advertisement in *El Mercurio.*

GEORGE: Another advertisement. What for?

ESTELA: What a question! Everything is all right now. No more fear of the Last Judgment. An angel passed through our house. But don't you realize? We still don't have a servant.

QUICK CURTAIN

CHECKLIST OF TRANSLATIONS

OF SPANISH AMERICAN PLAYS

arranged alphabetically by countries and
by names of dramatists

IT HAS BEEN DIFFICULT to obtain biographical data relating to the dramatists. Some of the entries listed below are therefore incomplete. The Library of Congress and the British Museum no longer include dates on their catalog cards and Latin American materials presently available show some unevenness in this respect.

Many of the translations listed below have not been published and are filed in manuscript form in the repositories indicated.

Argentina

Bayón Herrera, Luis. *Santos Vega* in Bierstadt *Three Plays of the Argentine.* New York: Duffield, 1920, pp. 21–75.
———. *The Straight Line.* Tr. anon. in *Inter-America,* 4 (1920), 56–68.
Cuzzani, Augustín (1924—). *Sempronio.* Tr. Roberto Sánchez. "Love vs. Atom Bombs." MS at Play Circle, University of Wisconsin.

Dragún, Osvaldo (1929––). "And They Told Us We Were Immortal." Three-act tragedy about youth in war and peace. Tr. Alden J. Green. MS at Pan-American Society of New England.

Gorostiza, Carlos (1920––). "The Bridge." Three-act clash of classes. Tr. Luis L. Curcio. MS at Pan-American Society of New England.

Gutiérrez, Eduardo (1835–90) and José Podestá (1856–1937). *Juan Moreira.* Tr. W. K. Jones and Carlos Escudero in *Poet Lore,* 51 (1945), 101–17; excerpts in Jones, *Spanish American Literature in Translation.* Vol. 2. *Since 1888.* New York: Ungar, 1963, pp. 371–79.

Leguizamón, Martianiano (1858–1935). *Calandria.* Three-act gaucho drama. Tr. from the Spanish in *Hispanic Notes and Monographs.* Hispanic Society of America, 1932.

Manco, Silverio. *Juan Moreira.* Two-act tragedy in Bierstadt *Three Plays of the Argentine,* pp. 1–19.

Méndez Calzada, Enrique (1898–1940). *Criminal.* One-act tragedy. Tr. anon. in *Inter-America,* 7 (1923), 115–25.

Payró, Roberto K. (1867–1928). *The Tragic Song.* One-act drama. Tr. W. K. Jones and Carlos Escudero in *Poet Lore,* 50 (1944), 3–24.

Pico, Pedro (1882–1945). *Common Clay.* One-act tragedy. Tr. W. K. Jones in *Short Plays of the Southern Americas.* Stanford University Press, 1944, pp. 55–69.

––––––. *You Can't Fool With Love.* One-act farce. Tr. W. K. Jones and Carlos Escudero in *Poet Lore,* 49 (1943), 107–34.

Rojas, Ricardo (1882–1957). *Ollantay.* Four-act tragedy. Excerpts tr. Angel Flores in *Bulletin of Pan-American Union,* 74 (March 1940), 149–53; also excerpts tr. E. J. R. Isaacs in *Theater Arts,* 24, No. 4 (April 1940), 252–56.

Sánchez Gardel, Julio (1879–1937). *The Witches Mountain.*

Three-act tragedy in Bierstadt *Three Plays of the Argentine,* pp. 77–130.

Bolivia

More, Federico (1889—). *Interlude.* One-act symbolic drama. Tr. Audrey Alden in F. Shay and Pierre Loving *Fifty Contemporary One Act Plays.* Cincinnati: Stewart and Kidd, 1922, pp. 39–44. Reprinted New York: Century, 1935; Cleveland: World, 1946.

Chile

Acevedo Hernández, Antonio (1886–1962). *Cabrerita.* One-act tragedy. Tr. W. E. Barclay in Alfred Coester *Plays of the Southern Americas.* Stanford University Press, 1943.
————. *Chañarcillo.* One act tragedy in Jones *Since 1888.*
Aguirre, Isidora (1919—). *Express for Santiago.* One-act comedy. Tr. Stanley Richards in Margaret Mayorga *Best Short Plays of 1959–60.* New York: Dodd, Mead, 1961, pp. 195–214.
————. *The Three Pascualas.* Three-act tragedy. Tr. W. K. Jones in *Poet Lore,* 59 (1965) ; excerpt in *Since 1888,* pp. 423–29.
Barrios, Eduardo (1884–1963). *For the Sake of a Good Reputation.* One-act farce. Tr. W. K. Jones in *Short Plays of the Southern Americas,* pp. 1–11.
————. *Papa and Mama.* Comic dialog. Tr. W. K. Jones in *Poet Lore,* 33 (1922) , 286–90.
Marín, Juan (1897—). *Orestes and I.* Three-act tragedy. Excerpt in *Before 1888,* pp. 331–34.
Marín, Juan (1897—). *Orestes and I.* Three-act tragedy. Tr. R. P. Butrick. Tokyo: Asia America, 1940.
Moock, Armando (1894–1942). *Don Juan's Women.* One-

act comedy. Tr. W. K. Jones in *Poet Lore,* 46 (1940), 47–75.

——. *Songbook of the Baby Jesus.* One-act comedy. Tr. W. K. Jones in *Poet Lore,* 45 (1934), pp. 23–53.

Roepke, Gabriela (1920—). "The Dangers of Great Literature." Tr. Thomas and Mary Patterson. MS at Pan-American Society of New England.

——. *The White Butterfly.* One act. Tr. Thomas and Mary Patterson in Margaret Mayorga *Best Short Plays of 1959–60,* pp. 145–64.

Vial y Ureta, Román (1833–96). *A Popular Election.* One-act satire in *Before 1888,* pp. 341–43.

Wolff, Egon Raúl (1926—). "The Invaders." Three-act nightmare. Tr. Margaret S. Peden. MS at Pan-American Society of New England.

Colombia

Buenaventura, Enrique (1925—). "Leaves from Hell." Tr. José Barba-Martín and Louis E. Roberts. MS at Pan-American Society of New England.

Zalamea, Jorge (1905—). *The Inn of Bethlehem.* One-act Nativity story in *Short Plays of the Southern Americas,* pp. 97–106.

Cuba

Cid Pérez, José (1906—). "His Final Conquest." Tr. Kenneth Chastain and Edward Mullen. MS at Purdue University.

——. *The Comedy of the Dead.* Tr. John P. Dyson in *First Stage.* Purdue University Press, 1967.

——. *Men of Two Worlds.* Tr. Mary H. Jackson in *Northwest Missouri State College Bulletin,* 1966.

Gómez de Avellaneda, Gertrudis (1814–73). *Belshazzar.* Four-act tragedy. Tr. Wm. F. Burbank. London: Stevens and Brown, and San Francisco: Robertson, 1914. Excerpts in *Poet Lore,* 17 (1901), 118–38 and in *Before 1888,* pp. 340–54.

Martí, José (1853–95). *Love is Repaid by Love.* One-act comedy. Tr. W. K. Jones in *Archivos de José Martí,* 2 (1947), 50–60.

Matas, Julio (1931—). "The Happening and its Account." Tr. Violet Frederick and Rodolfo Cardona. MS at Pan-American Society of New England.

Ramos, José Antonio (1885–1946). *The Traitor.* One-act tragedy of Cuban Revolution. Tr. W. K. Jones in *Short Plays from the Southern Americas,* pp. 12–24.

———. *When Love Dies.* One-act drama. Tr. Isaac Goldberg in Frank Shay *Twenty-Five Short Plays.* New York: Appleton, 1925, pp. 125–46.

Triana, José. "The Criminals." Three act "theatre of cruelty." Brandeis University performing manuscript at Pan-American Society of New England.

Ecuador

Aguilera Malta, Demetrio (1909—) and Willis K. Jones (1895—). *Blue Blood.* Three-act comedy. Washington, D. C.: Pan-American Union, 1948. Also published in Spanish and Portuguese.

Rendón, Victor (1859–1940). *The Lottery Ticket.* One-act children's play. Tr. W. K. Jones in *Short Plays of the Southern Americas,* pp. 47–54.

Guatemala

Anon. *Rabinal achí.* Tr. Eleanor Wolff in *Mesa,* 1 (1945) 4–18. Excerpts in *Spanish American Literature in*

Translation. Vol. 1. *Before 1888.* New York: Ungar, 1966, pp. 287–92.

Drago-Bracco, Adolfo (1894—) . *Colombine Wants Flowers.* One-act comedy. Tr. W. K. Jones in *Poet Lore,* 55 (1950) , 142–62.

Solórzano, Carlos (1922—) . "The Hands of God." Three-act anti-clerical play of oppression. Tr. W. Keith Leonard and Mario T. Soria. MS at Pan-American Society of New England.

Mexico

Anon. *Los Pastores.* Fifteenth-century Christmas play. Tr. M. R. Cole in *American Folklore Society Memoirs,* 9 (1907) ; and published by Houghton Mifflin, 1907. Version by the Griego family of Santa Fe, New Mexico recorded and translated by Mary E. Van Stone. Cleveland: Gates Press, 1933.

Anon. *Coloquios de los pastores.* Comp. and tr. Aurora Lucero White with music by Alejandro Flores. Library of Congress, 1940.

Anon. *The Shepherds' Play of the Prodigal Son.* Tr. George C. Barker. Berkeley: University of California Press, and London: Cambridge University Press, 1953.

Anon. *Passion Play of Tzintzuntzan.* Tr. Frances Toor in *Mexican Folkways,* 1 (1925) 21 ff.

Anon. *Los Tostones.* Tr. Frederick Starr in *Journal of American Folklore,* 15 (1902) , 73–83.

Cantón, Wilberto (1923—) . "We Are God." Drama of 1910 Mexican Revolution. Tr. S. Sam Trifilo. MS at Spanish Department, Marquette University.

Carballido, Emilio (1925—) . "The Golden Thread." Three acts. Tr. Margaret S. Peden. MS at Pan-American Society of New England. This and other Carballido plays eventually to be published in book form.

Carballido, Emilio (1925—). "Medusa." Tr. Mary Vázquez
Amaval. MS at Pan-American Society of New England.

Chavero, Alfredo (1841–1906). *Xochitl.* Excerpts tr. Frederick Starr in *Readings from Modern Mexican Authors.*
Chicago: Open Court Publishing Co., 1904, pp. 63 ff.

Farías de Issasi, Teresa (1878—). *The Sentence of Death.*
One-act tragedy. Tr. Lilian Saunders in Frank Shay
Twenty-Five Short Plays, pp. 273–81.

Gamboa, José Joaquín (1878–1931). "The Knight, Death,
and the Devil." Three-act tragedy. Tr. Theodore Apstein. Unpublished M.A. thesis, University of Texas,
Austin, 1937.

———. *An Old Yarn.* One-act comedy. Tr. W. K. Jones in
Short Plays of the Southern Americas, pp. 70–75.

Gorostiza, Celestino (1904—). "The Color of Our Skin."
Tr. S. Sam Trifilo. MS at Spanish Department, Marquette University.

Jiménez Rueda, Julio (1876–1960). *The Unforeseen.* Three-
act tragedy. Tr. Gino di Solemni in *Poet Lore,* 35
(1924), 1–24.

Monterde, Francisco M. (1894—). *She Who Returns to
Life.* Three-act comedy. Tr. Louis G. Zelson in *Poet
Lore,* 55 (1950), 291–335.

Navarro, Francisco (1902—). *The City.* One-act tragedy.
Pt. 1 of a trilogy. Tr. W. K. Jones in *Poet Lore,* 54
(1948), 72–82.

Novo, Salvador (1904—). *Eight Column Banner Spread.*
Three-act comedy. Tr. W. K. Jones in *Poet Lore,* 60
(1966), 25–80.

Orozco Rosales, Efrán. *El mensajero del sol.* Drama in bilingual edition. Mexico: Secretaría de Gobernación, 1941.

Peón Contreras, José (1843–1907). *Gil González de Avila.*
One-act classical tragedy in *Before 1888.*

———. *To Heaven.* Three-act colonial drama. Excerpts in
F. Starr *Readings from Modern Mexican Authors.* Chicago: Open Court Publishing Co., 1904.

Ruiz de Alarcón, Juan (1581–1639). *The Lying Lover or the Ladies' Friendship.* Five-act comedy. Adapted by Sir Richard Steele. London: Lintot, 1704.

———. *The Truth Suspected.* Five-act comedy. Tr. Julio del Toro and Robert V. Finney in *Poet Lore,* 30 (1927), 475–530. Also tr. Robert C. Ryan in Angel Flores *Spanish Drama.* New York: Bantam Press, 1962, pp. 139–89.

Saavedra y Bessey, Rafael. *La chinita.* Two acts. Tr. Lilian Saunders in *Poet Lore,* 37 (1926), 107–19.

Sor Juana Inés de la Cruz (1648–95). "Loa" from *Divine Narcissus.* Tr. W. K. Jones in *Before 1888,* pp. 300–308.

Souza, Antonio. *Pascualina, a Playlet* in *Américas,* 9, No. 12 (Dec. 1957), 21–25.

Usigli, Rodolfo (1905—). *Another Springtime.* Three-act drama. Tr. Wayne Wolfe. New York: Samuel French, 1961.

———. *Crown of Shadows.* Three-act drama. Tr. W. F. Sterling. London: Wingate, 1940. Act III in *Since 1888,* pp. 440–46.

Villaseñor Ángeles, Eduardo. *Chinese Coffee Shop.* One-act comedy. Tr. Howard S. Phillips in *Mexican Life.* 9 (September 1927), 23–24.

Villaurrutia, Xavier (1903–50). *The Hour Has Come.* One-act drama. Tr. Edna Lue Furness in *Odyssey Review,* 2 (1962), 88–98.

———. *What Are You Thinking About?* One-act comedy in *Odyssey Review,* 2 (1962), 68–87. Also tr. Lysander Kemp in *New World Writing,* 14 (1959).

New Mexico

Anon. *The Comanche Indians.* One-act drama of New Mexico Spaniards' defeat of Indians. Tr. A. M. Espinosa and J. M. Espinosa in *New Mexico Quarterly,* 1 (1931), 133–46.

Anon. *Coloquios de los pastores.* Comp. and tr. Aurora
Lucero White with music by Alejandro Flores. Library
of Congress, 1940.

Anon. "Los Pastores from Corpus Christi." M.S. thesis of
Mai Francis Hunter. Corpus Christi College of Arts and
Industries, 1940.

Anon. *Song of the Lost Child.* Seventeenth-century Lenten
folkplay of the Penitentes. Tr. Mary R. Van Stone and
E. R. Sims in *Spur of the Cock*, 11 (1933), 44–89.

Anon. *The Texans.* Defeat of Texas Invasion expedition of
1841. One act. Tr. Aurelio M. Espinosa and J. M.
Espinosa in *New Mexican Quarterly*, Autumn 1942, pp.
299–308.

Nicaragua

Anon. *The Güegüences* (Old Men) : *A Comedy Ballet in
the Nahuatl Dialect of Nicaragua.* Ed. and tr. Daniel G.
Brinton. Philadelphia: Brinton Press, 1883. 84 pp., par-
allel texts.

Peru

Anon. *Ollantay: An Ancient Inca Drama.* Tr. from Quechua
by Clements R. Markham. London: Trübner, 1871; also
in Markham, *The Incas of Peru.* London: Dent, and
New York: Dutton, 1910. Excerpts in *Pan-American
Magazine*, 33 (1921) 281–90; in E. C. Hills, *Hispanic
Studies.* Stanford University Press, 1929. Pp. 48 ff; and
in *Before 1888,* pp. 297–300.

Segura, Manuel Ascensio (1805–71). *Sergeant Canuto.* One-
act comedy. Tr. W. K. Jones in *Short Plays of the
Southern Americas,* pp. 25–46.

Philippines

Florentino, Alberto S., ed. *Outstanding Filipino Short Plays.* Manila: Filipiniana Publications, 1961. Distributed by Bookmark, Manila.

Puerto Rico

Marqués, René (1919—). *The House of the Setting Sun.* Three-act tragedy. Tr. W. K. Jones in *Poet Lore,* 59 (1965), 99–131. Excerpts in *Since 1888,* pp. 459–64.

Uruguay

Pérez Petit, Victor (1871–1946). *Moonlight Sonata.* One-act drama. Tr. W. K. Jones and Carlos Escudero in *Poet Lore,* 51 (1945), 353–67.

Sánchez, Florencio (1875–1910). *Representative Plays of Florencio Sánchez.* Tr. W. K. Jones. Pan-American Union, 1961.

———. *Down the Gully.* Excerpts in *Since 1888.*

———. *The Foreign Girl.* Tr. Alfred Coester in *Plays of the Southern Americas,* pp. 1–46.

———. *Mid-Summer Day Partners.* One-act sainete. Tr. W. K. Jones in *Short Plays of the Southern Americas,* pp. 76–96.

———. *Los Muertos.* Three-act tragedy. Tr. F. B. Luquiens in *Yale Review,* 17 (1928), 551–62.

Venezuela

Chocrón, Isaac (1932—). *Asia and the Far East.* Tr. Barbara Jardine. MSS of this and another performance version by Minneapolis' St. Paul's East Side Theater at Pan-American Society of New England.

Sources

Pan-American Society of New England. Mrs. Gardner Read, Director, 75a Newbury Street, Boston, Massachusetts, 02116. Source for a number of unpublished translations of Latin American and Brazilian plays in MSS.

Play Translation Center. Murphy Hall, 356F, The University of Kansas, Lawrence, Kansas, 66044. Being established as source for Latin American plays.

Bierstadt, E. H. *Three Plays of the Argentine*. New York: Duffield, 1920. Edition of translations by Fassett.

Coester, Alfred, ed. *Plays of the Southern Americas*. Stanford University Press, 1942. Eight translated plays.

Jones, W. K., ed. *Short Plays of the Southern Americas*. Stanford University: Dramatists Alliance, 1944. Eight plays in mimeograph.

Jones, W. K. *Short Spanish American Plays in English: 1519–1959*. Barron's Educational Series, 1970. Twenty plays illustrating the development of the Spanish American drama.

———. *Spanish American Literature in Translation*. Vol. 1. *Before 1888*. New York: Frederick Ungar, 1966. Excerpts from eleven plays.

———. *Spanish American Literature in Translation*. Vol. 2. *Since 1888*. New York: Ungar, 1963. Excerpts from fifteen plays.